the WATER CODE

UNLOCKING THE TRUTH WITHIN

Rainey Marie Highley

Published in the United States by
Divine Macroverse LLC
Houston, Texas

All images by Ryan Bache (www.bachedesign.com) except where otherwise noted.

Cover by Ryan Bache.
Diamond cover art, Clark Hawgood,
www.clarkhawgood.com

Full-color versions of all images can be found on the author's website:

www.raineymariehighley.com

ISBN: 1468011650

ISBN-13: 9781468011654

Library of Congress Control Number: 2011961918

First Edition

Published in the United States by
Divine Macroverse LLC
Houston, Texas

To the dolphins and whales,
gatekeepers and guardians of Earth's Akashic wisdom,
who have served as a bridge between water and humans
until such time when the collective vibration of humanity
was prepared for the release of these records.
That time is now.

CONTENTS

PART THREE: THE WATER CODE REVEALED

Preface

TRUTH IS FREEDOM

We are spiritual beings incarnated on Earth at this time for a reason.
Our time has come and our real work is beginning—
the work of assisting our Earth
through the unfolding Transformation.[1]

If you are familiar with my previous book, *Divine Macroverse,* you know that I am blessed with a wonderful relationship with a group of multidimensional beings known as the Macroversal Council. People sometimes ask if I channel the council and I am often hesitant to say yes. Channeling means different things to different people. To me, it implies a passive act, as if the channeler is an unconscious conduit for information that moves from other dimensions to this dimension. My experience with the council is much different because their messages are conveyed to me all at once, in an instant. It then becomes my responsibility to consciously translate the material from the language of light into human vocabulary. Similar to a seed containing all the ingredients to become a tree, I am given a seed containing all the

1 Joan Ocean, *Dolphins into the Future,* (Kailua, HI: Dolphin Connection, 1997), 181.

information to become a book. However, just as a tree's seed must be watered, cultivated, and nurtured in order to grow, ideas must be simplified, refined, and organized to manifest into a book. Therefore, I find the term "interdimensional communicator" much more accurate than "channeler" in describing my relationship with the council.

The information for this book came primarily from one member of the council called REMI. He uses this name for identification because, as he reminds me, our human vocabulary carries with it the limitations of space and time. In other dimensions, the need for names, identifying locations, or genders as we understand them are unnecessary. I have also found that beings in the higher frequencies operate in unity consciousness more than humans, which is why they prefer to speak with the pronoun "we" as opposed to "I." In this book, REMI appeased my need for individual description by using "I" in the introduction and the Q&A chapter at the end. However, he asked that "we" be used throughout the book, not only because he was speaking as a representative for water but also to reflect the energy of oneness that exists in the higher realms.

When *The Water Code* came into my conscious perception, I was overwhelmed by the sheer volume and complexity of the material presented. The message I received contained scientific insights from beings millions of years more advanced than us humans. Wait a second, I wondered, why are you communicating this information through me? I am a writer, a lawyer, an intuitive, yes, but certainly not a scientist! The answer they shared was clear: it was essential that I did not have any scientific training in order to maintain an open and receptive mind to material that may not align with the views of modern science. When I discovered that a significant portion of the book's message dealt with the quantum realms, I must admit, I went back to the council to double check, asking, "Are you sure you have the right person? I do not even know what 'quantum' means!" They had a good laugh over this and reassured me that yes, this information was to come into form through me. They also pointed out, on a number of occasions, that the more advanced a scientific concept is, the simpler it is to understand. Of course, this is the opposite of what I was taught in school. However, as I continued writing *The Water Code*, I was relieved to find that what they said was true. They presented the information clearly and simply while at the same time never taking anything away from the magnitude of these innovative concepts. As I discovered that the purpose of the book was to teach us how to access Truth directly, I knew I needed to get this information out into the world as quickly as possible.

One of the most influential books I have ever read was Barbara Marciniak's *Family of Light*. The book contains a message from the Pleiadians who focus quite a bit on the concept of Truth. They also provide the best definition for the word that I have ever heard:

Truth is where no secrets are kept. That is Truth.[2]

Do we have Truth in our present reality? The answer to this question certainly *seems* to be no as we are faced with disinformation, secrets, deceit and even lies. However, I have come to believe that this collective reality is a mere facade, temporarily veiling us from our true inheritance—that of Freedom, Respect, Compassion, and of course, Truth. For what is existence without these principles? Truth cannot be *kept* from us, for Truth lives within us, in every single molecule and cell of our being. This is the Key that REMI and the council share with us in this book, which shows how to unlock the Truth inside of us. As you may remember from *Divine Macroverse*, the council introduced the 13 Dimensions of All That Is, or what some refer to as the "Ocean of Light." In fact, the sacred geometric structure of light is the infinity symbol:

2 Barbara Marciniak, *Family of Light*, (Rochester, VT: Bear & Company Publishing, 1999), 197.

Clark Hawgood, *Light Infinity* (2011), www.clarkhawgood.com

In this Ocean of Light we call the Macroverse, the 13 Dimensions of Being are expressed as infinity symbols inside of infinity symbols:

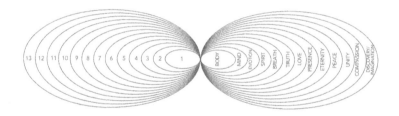

This shape represents the movement of light—the expression of being—like wings of a butterfly brushing against the canvas of existence. The exploration of All That Is has led us into the unlit corridors of the imagination and revealed infinite realities for us to experience. In our voyage into the 13 Dimensions of Being, we have gained valuable knowledge about our multidimensional selves. Now, it is time to turn inward and reflect upon the intricacies of impression as we journey into the quantum realms of our inner being. This shift in focus allows us to explore the companion to light, which is water.

What we know of water at this present moment is but a mere fraction of its vastness and complexity. Its genius, purity, and ancient wisdom extend well beyond the present understanding of our conscious minds. We have reached an exciting milestone in our collective development—a moment when the floodgates of Truth are thrown open as we reconnect with the magnificence of water. For eons of Earth years and even before the beginning of time, water has acted as the record keeper of Earth's Akashic Library, the great "computer" of creation and the encyclopedia of *every*thing and *no*thing.

The Water Code reveals that the sacred geometric structure of water is a diamond.

Clark Hawgood, *Water Essence* (2011), www.clarkhawgood.com

Water introduces us to the 9 Inner Realms of Non-Being, otherwise known as the *Micro*verse. This is represented in the image of 9 interlocking diamonds:

It is now, at this sacred moment in human history, that the two fundamental substances and structures of existence must be brought together in harmonious interrelationship:

This is the purpose of *The Water Code* and the essence of our next evolutionary step— transformation through harmony. It calls for a balanced knowledge of the Macroverse and the Microverse. It reunites the primordial substances of creation—water and light. Once this reunion has been realized, we will better understand the fundamental principles of our existence: Freedom, Truth, Respect and Compassion. While *Divine Macroverse* focused on awakening to Freedom, *The Water Code* focuses on unlocking the Truth. The book reveals the sacred geometric Key needed to unlock the records stored inside our bodies, in the inner realms of our water molecules. Once we hold the Key, Truth can never be kept from us again. And once we have Truth, we will also have Freedom. For Truth *is* Freedom.

May this book unlock the Water Code within you, opening you to the fullness of Truth that is the birthright of your essence and the resonant vibration that calls you Home.

In harmony with the principles of Freedom, Truth, Respect, and Compassion,

Rainey

Introduction

WATER'S AMBASSADOR

It is best to start with the truth. As a matter of fact—
if there is such a thing—it is best to end with the truth as well.[3]

Clark Hawgood, *Water Dragon* (2011), www.clarkhawgood.com

---

3 Barbara Marciniak, *Family of Light*, (Rochester, VT: Bear & Company Publishing, 1999), xviii.

XVII

Greetings to you, dear ones. My name is REMI and I am a water guide. I come to you now to share the full story of water. Although you have coexisted on this planet for eons, you do not yet really know water. You perceive a need for constant "hydration," as you call it, but have not yet recognized the vast intelligence of water or learned to consciously communicate with it. Water is a life form, just as humans are a life form. You could say that I am a "water being" just as you are a "human being." In fact, some may say that I am a Water Dragon. I come to you in this moment as an ambassador of water. As water's ambassador, I represent the highest path of water for the greatest good of All That Is. Because I speak on behalf of water, I will use the pronoun "we" instead of "I" throughout the book, with the exception of this Introduction and the Q&A chapter.

The time has come in human evolutionary development to know the truth about water and, in doing so, to learn the truth about yourselves. It is my intention in this book to reveal many things to you. These things you know in your heart to be true though they have been hidden from your conscious perception. In human vocabulary you might say that water exists far in the future and yet is quite ancient at the same time. If you really think about it, it may not be surprising to learn that water is the most advanced evolutionary life form on Planet Earth at this time. Much of the magnificence of water still remains a mystery to modern science. You know that all life requires water to survive. Do you know why this is? When you search for life on other planets or throughout the universe, what is the one thing you look for? Water, of course. You know that your bodies are comprised mostly of water. You also know that water is the consummate survivor. Although water is always moving, always transforming, it can never be destroyed. Your written records only date back a few thousand years, but water has observed *everything* on this planet for billions of years. Water is the great record keeper of Earth and, in fact, holds the Akashic Records of the planet within each molecule. Does it not make sense that instead of keeping Earth's records on stone tablets or paper scrolls, the planet's complete history would be preserved inside the one thing on Earth that can never be destroyed? Thus, it is an act of true wisdom and great significance to better understand this highly advanced life form known as "water." For water holds the Key to *all* information. In fact, water is much more than a gatekeeper to the Akashic Records. Water is *Truth*.

You may wonder why Truth has been veiled from humans for so long. Soon you will remember that the Macroverse itself has learned great lessons on Freedom and the nature of free will. These lessons have taught us that information is revealed only to those who are energetically ready to receive it. This protects the integrity of information itself and the freedom of those potentially affected by the misuse of such information. Because of the Macroversal principles of Freedom, Truth, Respect, and Compassion, humans historically have not been capable of relating to water or gaining access to the information held within it. Water has guarded and safely protected Earth's Akashic Library, knowing some day you would be ready to receive it. Thus, you could say that water itself was coded to release this information to you once you obtained energetic resonance with it. That time is now.

As you unlock the Water Code inside the water molecules within yourself, you will learn that water holds the Key to the Microverse, or the inner realms. Understanding these quantum realms is a necessary step in human evolution. Every step in Earth's development can be represented by a sacred geometric pattern. The Key to unlocking the Water Code is a sacred geometric pattern revealed to you in this book. Understanding and integrating this pattern into your being prepares you for the next step of evolutionary progression, both collectively and individually. May this sacred geometric Key to Truth awaken you to the fullness of your being and non-being, easing you into the vast and expansive Freedom of existence. Let the Truth remind you that, like the dragon, the fundamental emergence of all life resides within light and water.

Namaste.

PART ONE:
THE INTELLIGENCE OF WATER

1

THE MAGNIFICENCE OF WATER

*I am often asked, "What words did you use to create
the most beautiful crystal you've ever photographed?"
And my answer without hesitation is always,
"Love and gratitude."*[4]

We begin this book with love and gratitude. We send love to all of the incarnated Lightworkers on Planet Earth who have dedicated their lives to the service of the highest good of All That Is. We are grateful for your compassion, your bravery, your sacrifice, and your endurance. We are honored to know you, to call you our family, and now to share these Truths with you. We commence with love and gratitude for another reason. Your body is composed of water, and it is our intent to reach a resonant frequency with the molecules of water comprising your body. We ask you to send love and gratitude to the water within you, recognizing the harmonious interconnection that is created in this energetic expression. For it is in the spirit of Harmony and the vibration of Truth that we begin our story.

4 Masaru Emoto, *The Miracle of Water* (New York, NY: Atria Paperback, 2007) ix.

The Origin of Water

We share with you the story of our origins, for they are also your origins. We invite you to know the Truth of who you are, where you came from, and what you are made of. We will start at the beginning while at the same time reminding you that there is no beginning or end, or time, for that matter. You could say time is an illusion, although we prefer to think of it as a matter of perception. With this in mind, let us journey back before the beginning. Before time, before space, before individual life and Consciousness, all that was existed as one in a state of complete being-ness. We call this existence. You may wonder if existence has always been, and we would ask that you try to understand the beginning in eternal terms and not as a "before and after" timeline. Existence is and was and always will be, farther than we can see. Being is the core. It is beyond reach. It is who we are. It flows through all of us. It is the tie that binds us, the thread weaving us through the fabric of eternity. It is within and without, the beyond the beyond. Many great sages have asked, what was *before* existence? What is beyond being-ness? We believe the question is in and of itself flawed. There is no separation, you see. For it is all Source. By definition, the Source is where everything comes from and where everything flows back to instinctively. For just as we are Consciousness, we are also Source. The individual and the infinite are always expanding and exploring, basking in the joyous energy of creative expression.

To provide you with an overview, we would say that Source is simply and magnificently the Ocean of Light we refer to as All That Is. It was from this ocean that Consciousness emerged with the intention to experience the act of creation and the energy of love. This desire led to what we call the "expressions of Consciousness." Water was the first expression of Consciousness and fire was the second. We call them Primordial Water and Primordial Fire. From these two fundamental substances, all life was created. All creation is born from Source, yes, but we also all have a creator. A string of creative action binds us together and, if you follow the string, you will return to the Prime Creator, or the Consciousness of Source.

The Form of Water

Following the initial expressions of Consciousness, Prime Creator manifested the experience of form by utilizing the energy of fire and the coding of water. The life form known as water on Earth is somewhat different from its primordial expression, primarily so it can reach a resonant frequency, allowing it to manifest physically on the planet. Water is an integral part of Earth and all life on the planet, yet water retains its mystery because so little is consciously known about it. We intend to reveal to you the Truth about water, and in doing so, reveal the Truth of who you are, where you come from, and ultimately, where you are going. What you may not yet realize is that water is an intelligent life form—by "intelligent" we mean *much* more intelligent than any other life form on Planet Earth at this time.

Water is a quiet observer of Earth's history. Water cannot be invaded or manipulated, for its physical design provides itself complete protection from harm and destruction. This is quite unlike the human form, which is very susceptible to sickness, disease, and of course death. You could say that water is a very advanced life form from millions of years in the future. So far in the future, in fact, that water is quite ancient. Water is so advanced that it is almost entirely unrecognizable to lower-frequency energies.

To give you a brief background, water is a highly evolved life form designed to withstand the whims of personality, the advances of technology, and the forces of nature that it may encounter. Thus, water can exist on a denser, more chaotic plane of life and yet continue to retain its vibratory sanctity and its alignment with the more refined planes of existence. As we said, water's purity always remains untouched. It may appear that there is a water crisis on Earth right now and indeed, there is. However, it is not a problem of contaminated water, for water cannot be contaminated. Instead, it is an issue of the invasion of sacred space on the outskirts of each water molecule's aura. So many toxins have been leaked, dumped and spilled into the water's living quarters that the space around each water molecule has become cloudy, contaminated, and masked. This dirty neighborhood that Earth's water calls home has become a veil between the vibration of water and the frequency of Earth and her inhabitants.

As water reveals its truth to you and reaches out to communicate with you, it asks that you raise your awareness to minimize the negative effect humans have on the planet and far beyond. Water wishes to establish a cooperative relationship with you. In exchange for your increased awareness, compassion, and for ultimately raising your collective vibratory frequency, water shall assist you in unlocking the code embedded within each water molecule in your body. Water will show you the Truth of who you are and will reveal the history of life on Planet Earth that has been hidden from you for so long. For it is only in understanding the Truth of who you are that you will be able to move forward into the full expression of who you are destined to become.

Blended Consciousness

Water transcends the current state of human consciousness because it exists in a dimension of blended consciousness. Humans are currently experiencing individual consciousness on the journey to remembering oneness consciousness. There is much discussion about what differentiates blended consciousness from oneness consciousness. We are reminded, however, that the very task of differentiating is an expression of separate consciousness. Thus, we satiate our desire to understand this by our acceptance of the vast array of life perspectives on this ever-evolving journey known as existence.

Instead of trying to "figure it out," we ask you to consider what it means to "blend." Blending does not require equal parts of everything, it implies a certain resonance of all parts to create a harmonious mixture. Blending is not only an act of unity but also an act of respect for the various vibrations represented by each ingredient. Blending accounts for individual strengths and weaknesses in an attempt to achieve harmonious balance. (Please excuse the duality of our vocabulary and know there is no judgment, only a true perspective.) Truth is considered fundamental, whereas "fairness," at least from a human perspective, is outweighed by the necessity for harmony. This is one of the great lessons of all of existence, and its significance is highlighted on Planet Earth right now. True harmony is the very definition of Freedom. Therefore, the vibration of intention must be considered in all blending. The reason blending is not working on Earth right now is because Earth's environment is a free-for-all in which those in power give no weight to intention. This has resulted in virus-like actions. Those with dominating energy who seek to infringe on others are being allowed to take by force from those with more harmonious intentions. It is a situation that results in disharmony and, ultimately, a lack of real Freedom for most everyone.

When we talk about change, we say it must start from the inside out. Take a moment to consider this as you take a drink of water. What better way to evolve the human form than through the mechanism of water? What better way to restore true Freedom? Sure, we have provided you with the tools to protect yourself and to manifest a safe world around you. However, it was also necessary to provide you with a tangible, physical demonstration of true Freedom. Now think about water molecules. They are perfectly defended in their molecular structure and integrity. Although their *environment* may suffer violations of Freedom such as pollution or toxicity, the *individual water molecules* are always protected. Their freedom cannot be invaded. Their integrity cannot be shaken. Their life experience cannot be interrupted. Thus, it makes perfect sense that just as Lightworkers came to Earth to ground light, defend Freedom and restore hope by changing Earth from the inside out, so too, did water come to this planet to ground light, defend Freedom, and restore hope in every individual body on Earth. As you drink water, it changes you from the inside out just as you are changing Planet Earth. Exciting, isn't it?

2

WATER—THE KEY TO ASCENSION

You follow the mist, and the mist envelops you
and you become one with it,
using the mist to travel into what the mist knows;
for the mist exists between you and the other worlds.[5]

As you may know, water is the only natural substance on Planet Earth able to transform from a solid to a liquid and to a gas within the normal range of planetary temperatures. No other substance on Earth is able to move between forms so effortlessly. Have you thought about what it means to be able to transform yourself? Have you considered the magnitude of what water is capable of achieving? Think about your body. Have you ever transformed your body into another physical form? Not yet, but you should know that this *is* possible. Consider the term "ascension." Ascension has been talked about by many of you. This is something you desire to experience, to achieve. But do you know what it means to ascend? Of course, there is "raising your vibration" and the subsequent evolutionary

---

5 Barbara Marciniak, *Family of Light*, (Rochester, VT: Bear & Company Publishing, 1999), 242.

advancement that accompanies such a shift. However, we would like you to consider that ascension means trans*form*ing. Like water, humans are capable of moving into another physical form.

If humans are made up mostly of water, and water is able to transform from a solid to a liquid to a gas, would it not seem logical that the human body is also capable of such transformation? In fact, all that is required is a unity of purpose, intent, and focus among the water molecules comprising the human body. Your key to transformation—to ascension—is your water. Now consider what conditions support the transformation of water. Temperature is quite important. When water is subjected to freezing temperatures, it forms a cohesive and static substance—ice. Ice represents a picture of water at a particular moment, like a photograph. It is solid, concrete, and it tells a story of something specific and identifiable. Now, as water is subjected to warmer temperatures, the ice starts melts and water experiences a freedom of movement far beyond its ability as an ice form. Water prefers to move as a group; its tendency is toward unification with its resonant frequency—other liquid water. Even raindrops find their way back to each other. A lone drop on a dry surface eventually evaporates, journeying back to the unified whole. This cohesive characteristic of water represents its innate understanding of the fundamental principle of all existence: we are all *one*. We are a unified whole, an expression of life-force energy that is always moving, always learning, always growing, always seeking new experiences. What a wonderful treat to watch this truth in action as we observe the brilliance of water.

Now consider what happens when water is subjected to high temperatures. It transitions from a liquid to a gas, moving from a unified whole to individual water particles like tiny, distinct bubbles traveling cohesively, yet independently. Similar to the movement of an ocean but with a bit more space between each water particle, water's form becomes a gas. Have you ever watched the water in your shower when the sun shines on it? It is quite remarkable. Liquid water moving with the flow of gravity down toward the shower drain transforms into minuscule steam droplets that look like dots in the air, moving *up* toward the light, outside of the dimension of gravity, beyond the rules of being in liquid form, and into a completely different realm. This new dimension has its own rules, and at this point in Earth's evolution, it can only be experienced through water. We are speaking of the dimension of mist, of magic, of myst-ery.

The Dimension of Mist

Mist occurs when water is impacted by warmer temperatures, and it is highly dynamic. Mist bubbles move so quickly and beautifully that they would appear to possess an oceanic or even smoke-like quality, dancing in and out of shapes like beautiful art, or liquid air. We are challenged to find words to describe the dimension of mist because this realm is as yet undiscovered, thus lacking descriptive terminology. So, mist is a contradiction of sorts. It is thick yet untouchable, chaotic yet calming, rapid yet lingering and mundane yet magical. It acts independently yet remains cohesive, enveloping everything while allowing all. It is an observable form of transcendence, reminding you of that which you are capable and what the future holds for you.

Mist is one of the most magical substances on the planet, yet it is quite unnoticed, almost unrecognized, by most. Mist is *the* most evolved form of water on the planet and yet its magnificence and power remain unseen by humans. You have surely given some attention to the perfection and beauty of bubbles. To humans, bubbles represent the movement of air through water. In actuality, a bubble is the movement of water through air within cohesive groupings of liquid water, although this can be difficult to see through physical vision. You have probably noticed a bubble floating through the air. Undoubtedly you have observed the stunning, multicolored, reflective nature of the bubble—beautiful and profound, yet apparently so delicate. Bubbles are in fact one of the most durable physical forms in the Macroverse. Earth's scientific community is very interested now in quantum phenomena, given the incredible influence of quantum physics on human understanding of third-dimensional life. In the quantum realms, bubbles are very resilient. Perfectly spherical and made entirely of water, bubbles are the most common transportation vehicle in the physical form. Right now, human society has only recently discovered the existence of the quantum planes. As you progress in your evolutionary development, you will explore the quantum realms. In this exploration, you will discover many fascinating Truths about these dimensions. So much exists here that all your discoveries may make you feel like your head is spinning. We do not want to spoil the surprise for you, but we will share with you an important truth: mist is the doorway to the quantum realms.

In fact, you could think of mist as a sort of celestial highway into the quantum realms. Consider the act of channeling, or interdimensional communication. To have a clear conversation, humans must close their eyes and go into meditative states. This requires the human being to journey inside the self to communicate with other realms. Why? You may wonder. Because higher vibrational light beings typically exist in the quantum dimensions. Therefore, humans must access the quantum realms to have such a meeting. You may find it surprising to learn that it is much easier to surf the mist than to meditate with the intent of reaching the astral planes. Meditation requires great focus of the mind and of the breath, nonthinking, nonjudgment, and nondoing. Interdimensional mist travel is much easier because it does not require focus. The mist holds the focus; all you must do is come along for the ride. Mist opens the senses and allows you to move into its unique frequency, perfect for travel and exploration.

Mist is profound in many ways, mainly because of its transformative and shape-shifting qualities. You will soon be able to distinguish between mist and gas. Fog is a gas. Steam is a mist. What is the main difference between a mist and a gas? Temperature conditions and vibratory signatures. Liquid water combined with high temperature conditions creates mist. Mist combined with cooler temperature conditions creates gas, such as fog. You have probably noticed that fog often lingers and has a quality of weight to it. It covers and surrounds. It rolls in and settles. It hovers and then dissipates. Mist has a much higher frequency, with a rapid and harmonic movement. Warmer temperatures cause the bubbles of mist to dance, moving like a flock of birds sailing gently on gusts of wind. In addition to temperature, you will discover that other conditions such as light, color, and sound contribute to the formation of mist. The dimension of mist is an exciting new frontier awaiting your exploration.

The Message in the Mist

As we mentioned, mist is created by elevated temperatures and has a high frequency, and therefore it becomes a gateway into the unseen realms. Have you looked at the mist in the sunlight? What does it show you? Do you see its constant, flowing, musical, and, of course, myst-ical movement? It reveals to you a doorway into the ocean—the Ocean of Light connecting all life in existence together and to the song of life. What you know you will see expanded in the mist, and what you feel will be enhanced by its lingering and potent magic. Acting as a gentle escort between realms, the mist releases you when you are born and receives you again upon death. The mist is the key to time travel and also beyond-time travel. You may wonder how mist and the quantum dimensions are related, and we would ask you to practice this exercise. Observe the mist. Really *look* inside of the mist. What do you see? Droplets of water? Tiny orbs of light? Does it look like millions of stars moving in oceanic harmony? What exists beyond that? The mist holds a message for you, but you must first change your beliefs about the communication of messages. Know that messages of a higher frequency come not in the form of words but in patterns of color, sound, light, and sacred geometry. Do you see the messages in the mist?

The mist carries within it many ancient secrets. These secrets were preserved, not surprisingly, in the realms of finer frequencies. Because of this, the secrets are protected from the densities of Earth's reality until a time when conditions have shifted. There is so much we will share with you, yet so much that has been left unsaid. Think for a moment about the concepts of hot and cold; of fire and ice. These conditions certainly have an effect on the experience, or the expression of water. Frozen water preserves a moment in a timeless space until such moment that it may be opened and its contents revealed within space and time. Frozen water is not active, at least not in the present moment. The addition of temperature conditions on water's third-dimensional expression create a mechanism for the preservation and release of information. For quite some time, temperature-impacted water has been used for keeping records and storing very sensitive information to protect it. In fact, many crystals act as storage devices for frozen water. This frozen water carries within it ancient secrets and important information for the transition of Earth into a quantum life experience interconnected with the whole of existence.

Imagination is the key to quantum understanding. The quantum fields are where much information resides. At this point in time you think of things in terms of size: this is larger than that, that is smaller than this. In truth, size is simply an expression of limitation, or of duality. What exists is neither larger nor smaller than something else. It exists in forms appropriate for its surroundings, and it exists in surroundings appropriate for its forms. What you should know is that the visible spectrum holds few of the answers you seek. This is another reason why life outside of your planet has been difficult to find. The life forms on Earth are quite primitive by comparison. Not many other life forms in the universe, or the Macroverse, still exist at this "size" and density. Really, it is a matter of frequency, and soon you will perceive this to be true. The patterns for quantum participation have been given to you like a recipe or sequence of codes. Look for these revelations in sacred geometric patterns, such as crop circles or patterns in nature. Life exists *everywhere,* just not at the same frequency, or density, as human life. Once you are able to travel into the quantum realms, all of life's mysteries will reveal themselves to you. The mist-story, or mystery, will be known.

3

WATER IS CODED TO COMMUNICATE

Water is condensed light and the highest form of intelligence.[6]

A s you now know, water is much more than a chemical compound or an essential element for life. It is intelligent, evolved, and sentient. In truth, its conscious awareness far surpasses that of human life on Earth at this time. This means that it possesses a perspective that is vastly more expansive and more advanced than the limited perception of current human understanding. You could say that water is all-knowing and all-seeing, and this would be true. As we said before, water *is* Truth. The purpose of this book is to reveal this Truth to you. To do so requires that you gain a more complete understanding of water as a highly evolved species and in turn grasp the exceptional opportunity to learn that water is offering you now. You are opening to the incredible transformative power of water, and you will continue to receive great delight from all you discover. For water is always moving, exploring, transforming, and communicating. In

---

6 Benoit Le Chevallier, founder of *Pangaea Project*, www.pangaeaproject.com, email message to author, August 4, 2011.

fact, water is quite powerful. It is true that water is an element necessary for life, but soon you will learn that it is also a great teacher. It contains within it the imprint of all things yet at the same time appears translucent, as if it contains nothing. Its greatness goes unnoticed by most of you on this planet, but soon you will understand more. If you can resonate with it, you will learn many powerful secrets.

You will remember from the book *Divine Macroverse* that a "harmony shield" is an energetic shield preventing nonresonant energies from entering a body's energy field, thus providing ultimate protection and complete individual Freedom. As a very advanced life form, water has perfected the use and control of its harmony shield, allowing it to exist on Earth yet remain totally untouchable by any inhabitant on the planet. Consider swimming or showering. You are covered in water, submerged in water, yet you never enter the energetic space of the water droplets. You dry off. The water leaves. It goes into a towel and disappears or you lay in the sun and soon it evaporates. Even the water absorbed into your body reconnects to the water coursing through your cells and eventually disappears through perspiration and elimination. Did you ever think about how incredible that is? Did you ever think about your body's need to drink eight glasses of water each day? If water retains its harmony shield to separate it from our bodies and Earth, you may wonder, why is it that you need water to regularly pass through your body. Why does all life on Earth require it? Is it an energetic imprint left behind by water? Is it simply to dispose of waste by washing it through your body? While all of these things are wonderful benefits of the movement of water through your system, none of them are the primary reason you need water. The significance of ingesting water into your body lies in the communicative power of water. Water is the universal, or we should say *Macroversal* translator. It has the ability to communicate with all life in the Macroverse and to translate that information to anyone or anything in existence. Water can link everything to everything else because it has the power to communicate with all life, regardless of substance, language, dimension, or fundamental element. You might say water speaks and understands all languages, for it reads energy and intention. Water is fluent in the language of essence.

When water moves through your body, it integrates itself into your cellular structure and takes stock of what is going on in every part of your body. It then communicates its observations to all the other molecules within your body, thereby providing a sort of coherence and optimization of the functioning of the body. Imagine that your liver was struggling with an overload of toxins. The liver's cells can send out a vibratory note to the rest of the body notifying other cells of the situation. However, a vibratory sounding such as this can be delayed in reaching other cells or even distorted when mixing with other vibratory frequencies along the way. The reason for this is that the harmony shield of a vibratory note is like most harmony shields on the planet at this time: it is not able to retain complete purity; thus it often experiences interference. The purest harmony shield on Earth, however, exists in water. Water is capable of instantaneous and undiluted communication with zero interference.

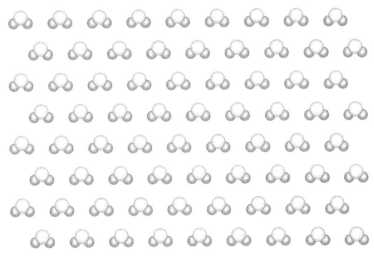

Therefore, when water moves through the body and discovers that the liver is overloaded with toxins, it sends out an immediate notification to all the cells in the body that the liver needs rapid assistance for detoxification. This unparalleled ability to instantaneously communicate makes water the ultimate healer to humans and to all life in the Macroverse.

Water is also the ultimate storehouse of Akashic information, for what is known by a single water molecule is known by all. Water molecules maintain constant and unbroken communication among each other. So, whatever information is gained by one water molecule is instantaneously shared among all water molecules, everywhere. You might think that a water molecule could "max out" from information overload, but that is not the case. The storage capacity of water is infinite. Therefore, it should come as no surprise that all of the information about all of Earth's incarnations is contained within every single molecule of water.

What You Know about Water

You know that water is the only substance on Earth to change from a solid to a liquid to a gas within the normal range of planetary temperatures. Now consider this. Water is the only *substance* to coexists simultaneously in all 13 dimensions of existence. In fact, water is the ultimate communicator, *the* Macroversal translator, and one of the most highly misunderstood substances on Earth at this time. Let us take a moment to reflect on what you know about water.

- Water is necessary for all life.
- More than 70 percent of the Earth is water.
- More than 70 percent of the human body is water.
- Humans require 6 to 8 glasses of water every day.
- Water molecules have a unique energetic imprint that can be captured when frozen (no two snowflakes are alike).
- Water has the ability to give life and also to destroy it through flooding, hurricanes, tidal waves, tsunamis, and other phenomena.
- Water is what scientists look for to identify where life may exist outside of Earth.

- Water regularly falls from the sky in the form of rain, snow, ice, fog, and mist.
- Water possesses reflective qualities. When you look into it, you see yourself.
- Water has the ability to amplify color.
- The harmonious blending of water and light creates some of the most spectacular beauty in the known world.
- Water transforms itself regularly. Not only does it transform from a solid to a liquid to a gas, but it can also transform into something different entirely. For example, when coffee beans or tea leaves are placed in hot water, the water transforms into a duplicate of the substance.
- Water removes waste and disharmonious energies from the body.
- Cold or room-temperature water is often used to dilute substances.

Please realize that these scientific facts represent about one percent of a thorough comprehension of water. Water transcends not only human understanding but most understanding of life throughout the Macroverse. Truly, entire libraries could be filled with books detailing the magnificence of water. It is time to expand the human perspective on water. It is our pleasure to introduce you to a more complete appreciation of one of the most magical substances in all of existence.

What You Don't Know about Water

Consider these new perspectives on water:

- **Water Is a Navigator.** Water is always aligned with the center of the Macroverse. It is somewhat like gravity—although water travels freely, it always leads you home. If you follow water, it will eventually take you to the center of your universe, then to the center of your dimension, until you reach the center of the Macroverse.

- **Water Is a Balancer.** It is an equal distributor. For example, if energy is misaligned, you could send in water to create an equilibrium. This is interesting in relation to Earth. Such vast amounts of water on Earth are intended to retain balance through these most energetically unstable times. Water works to neutralize unstable energy fields by sending out its own responsive harmonizing energies. This is why being near large bodies of water can make you feel balanced and peaceful.

- **Water Is a Translator.** Water has the ability to communicate with energies from all walks of life across vastly different planets and universes and throughout the 13 dimensions of existence. Water does not use language to communicate as you might think, given your third-dimensional perspective. Instead, water uses its reflective qualities to open up lines of communication. Consider the story of Columbus sailing to the New World and encountering the Native Americans, who of course appeared very foreign to Columbus and his men. How were communications initiated? Through a reflective-type sign language. Perhaps Columbus pointed to a flower and said, "flower" and the natives pointed to the same flower and said, "lomasi." Essentially, each tribe shared its interpretive vibratory signature for an object or idea. What is so fascinating about Dr. Masaru Emoto's initial findings in the Messages from Water series[7] is the fact that water reflects its own vibratory interpretation for each idea presented to it. So water interprets the word "beautiful" as a beautiful geometric pattern, whereas it interprets "evil" as an unattractive geometric pattern. What humans will soon realize is that water is introducing itself to you as an intelligent consciousness through this reflective communication process.

- **Water Is a Healer.** You will notice a correlation between drinking more water and having better health. Sickness is

---

7 Masaru Emoto, *Messages from Water*, vol. 1 (Hado Publishing, 1999); *Messages from Water*, vol. 2 (Sunmark Publishing, 2001); *The Hidden Messages in Water* (Beyond Words Publishing, 2004); *The Message from Water III: Love Thyself* (Hay House, 2006).

reduced, energy is gained. People feel better, look better, and even lose weight by drinking water. The reasons for this are not fully understood yet, but what humans will soon discover is that this is due to the fantastic healing capabilities of water.

- **Water Is a Transporter.** It is important to note how and why you arrived where you are today. Earth and all her inhabitants did not originate from one big bang. Many inhabitants of Earth originally arrived via frozen water. Frozen water acts as transportation device, preserving the integrity of the passenger while often traveling great distances or through extremely different climates, varying dimensional landscapes, and unexpected atmospheric conditions. This is one of water's unique and most identifiable qualities: it can transport from one destination to another, easily moving through any and all atmospheric and climatic conditions, while providing an unchanging environment for travel. The water "vehicle" is ideal for preserving and protecting cargo from outside conditions.

- **Water Is a Preserver.** Ice can preserve a moment intact for eons, with no limit. Think about that. In a reality enslaved by time, water has the ability to bypass third-dimensional laws of physics through the simple process of transformation into a solid. Soon you will learn that crystals are actually another form of water that has been preserved, which is why so many historical records have been kept inside the molecular structure of crystals.

- **Water Is a Record Keeper.** While crystals are similar to computer chips that store selected information, water molecules are the keepers of *all* information. Water is imprinted with all Truth and as such contains the Akashic Records for Earth and all life in the Macroverse. Because its form can never be destroyed, it was only natural that water would act as the ultimate storehouse of Macroversal information.

- **Water Is a Bridge.** Water has the unique ability to create a bridge between multiple realities, acting as the gatekeeper to other dimensions and other worlds. Learning to follow water is the key to all scientific discovery. The key to everything resides in water.

Three Stages of Conscious Communication

We ask you to carry this knowledge with you as you participate in Earth's Great Transformation—humanity's unprecedented evolutionary jump into a higher collective frequency. As this awakening occurs, much information is coming to light. Perhaps the most exciting news rests within the intelligence that is being offered to you by water. *The very step that will propel humanity into the reality of the new Earth resides in water.* Would you like to know how to cure disease, end suffering, and restore harmony to the environment on Earth? Water has all of these answers and more. We hope you understand the magnitude of what is being offered to you. Learning to communicate with water is equivalent to sitting down with a team of scientists from millions of years in the future. Just imagine how much there is to learn!

Due to the extensive evolutionary gap between humans and water, there is no common language to use for communication. Therefore, it is helpful to understand the Three Stages of Communication initiated by water.

1ST STAGE: IDENTIFICATION

This is an important stage in developing conscious communication. It involves the recognition of humankind and water as potentially resonant in frequency. When two species are far apart in evolutionary advancement or life experience, it may be difficult for them to even recognize each other as species with which they would like to communicate. Identifying the *possibility* for communicative contact is the first step in the communication process. Dr. Masaru Emoto's work made a significant leap forward for humanity by recognizing the sentient nature of water. Water has observed humanity since its inception on Earth. This book is an affirmation of your evolutionary progression by the species water.

2ND STAGE: REFLECTION

This stage of the communication process represents the first step of participatory communication between any two resonant species. Known as "Reflection," this stage involves a display of conscious awareness by both species. You point to the night sky and say, "moon." Another points to the same and says, "lune." Reflection represents the individual display of harmonic interpretation. It is the expression of *language*. This stage of communication has been documented extensively by Dr. Masaru Emoto in *Messages from Water.* He placed a word such as "Love" or "Gratitude" on containers filled with energetically neutral water. He then took a photo of the water in each container at a temperature of -5 degrees Celsius and discovered the water *responded* to the words by creating a corresponding geometric shape captured within its frozen crystalline structure. Put simply, the beautiful words (in any human language) produced beautiful crystals while the negative words produced unattractive crystals. This communication represents harmonic interpretation. The *intention of the word* was reflected by the water in a harmonic shape. This stage of communication displayed conscious awareness by water as well as its interpretative harmonic language. This was the first documented communication between modern humans and water and represents an effort on behalf of water to engage in conscious communication with you.

3RD STAGE: REVELATION

Now that water has established a point of communication with humanity through the process of Reflection, it is time for water to share its message with you. If you are reading this book, you are a human energetically prepared to receive this message. This is the stage we are engaged in now. Water contains within it Akashic wisdom that it would like to share with you now. Are you ready? Of course, water is not going to hand over written records for you to read, for this is not how information is preserved or translated in the higher frequencies. Every water molecule in your body possesses the records of *everything* within it. You could say that water is *coded* with information. It is ready to share that information with you. All you must do is learn to *receive* this information. We call this "unlocking the Water Code."

PART TWO:
UNLOCKING
THE WATER CODE

4

PREPARING TO RECEIVE: ESTABLISHING RESONANCE

Open your mind as you read our words for we speak to the library of knowledge inside of you.[8]

When we say that the answers are inside of you, what does that really mean? Is it simply a metaphor for knowing yourself better, or is it perhaps a technique for reaching a deeper state in meditation? We invite you to reconsider the meaning of these words. Existence is multidimensional, and there are layers inside of layers of meaning within everything. From our perspective, these words provide a literal roadmap to the library of all libraries awaiting your discovery inside the water molecules in your body. Water holds the answers you are seeking because water holds the Truth. As we have said before, water *is* Truth. Truth involves the accessibility of all perspectives and an inability to keep secrets. The reason you so deeply long for the Truth is because you are presently experiencing a collective reality

---

8 Barbara Marciniak, *Family of Light* (Rochester, VT: Bear & Company Publishing, 1999), 43.

from a limited perspective where it *seems* like you are separated from Truth. Just as your physical body requires water for survival, so too does your essence require Truth for continued existence. In fact, you might say that the human body's constant thirst for water is actually a thirst for the Truth. We are excited to tell you that this thirst will soon be quenched.

The Water Code inside your molecules is ready to reveal itself to you. What is required of you is receptivity and understanding. It is important to remember that information is received by those in resonance with information's vibration. In simple terms, like attracts like. For you to receive the Water Code inside of you, you must raise your vibratory frequency to establish a harmonious connection with water. Now that you understand the intelligence of water and recognize that it has reached out to communicate with humans, you are ready to take the steps to prepare your body for this communication. Once you have achieved vibratory resonance, water will provide you with the tools for unlocking the coded information inside your water molecules. Learning to access the storehouse of information contained within each water molecule inside your body is a process we call unlocking the Water Code. This is the simple key to your Truth. Therefore, we would like to offer the following suggestions for establishing resonance with the higher frequencies of water so you may easily receive the Water Code.

Drink Harmonized Water

What is the frequency of the water composing your human body in this moment? The answer depends on a variety of factors, but primarily, it is determined by the general frequency of the thoughts and emotions in your energy field, your environmental conditions, and the vibration of the substances you ingest. Many of you are quite careful about the foods you eat, opting for fresh, raw, and organic foods. You do this because you are considerate of the vibration of the foods you use as fuel for your body. You feel better, look better, and operate better physically when you make such choices. Most of you also choose to drink purified or spring water instead of tap water for the same reasons. This is certainly a wise choice, for you are moving from energetically *negative* water to energetically *neutral* water. However, it is a good idea to also *positively* energize the water you drink prior to ingestion.

Photo Credit: Naomi Arnold

We call this "harmonizing" your water. Harmonized water allows you to ingest water of a very high frequency into your body. This results in an overall increase in your vibratory rate, easily creating a resonance with the finest light and water frequencies available to you. Drinking harmonized water is essential to maintaining a high vibration. There are many ways to harmonize your water. To make your own "Harmony Water" we would suggest an intuitive combination of the following:

- Start with clean glass or crystal containers, preferably with lids or screw-on caps to keep the water free from contaminants.

- Place the containers in a location that receives direct sun and moonlight.

- Add a clean, energized crystal to each water container.*

Photo Credit: Naomi Arnold

---

* It is important to clean your crystals both physically and energetically. Salt water works very well to cleanse your crystals as does smudging with sage or sweetgrass. There are many ways to energetically prepare your crystals so follow your intuition to determine the best method for you.

Remember that crystals transfer information to the water, so be thoughtful in the crystals you select. Make certain to choose non-toxic, water-compatible crystals such as clear quartz, rose quartz, citrine, rainbow obsidian, lapis lazuli, diamond or amethyst.

- Add sacred geometric patterns, loving images or words to your water containers to "imprint" your water.

Photo Credit: Naomi Arnold

Because water's tendency is to harmonize with the energies surrounding it, you can positively energize your water by adding positive words or inspiring images to your water containers. You may select beautiful images from magazines or simply print inspiring patterns or images from your computer. Adhere these images to the side or bottom of the water container. Be creative in selecting images or words to use for your Harmony Water.

Copyright 2012 © Blue Bottle Love, www.bluebottlelove.com

- Fill your water containers with natural spring water such as FIJI Natural Artesian Water.

- Energize your water with color by using colored glass containers or adding colored images to your water pitcher.[9]

- Add your intention to the water by taking a moment to send love and gratitude or a special message to the water.

- Energize your water with sound by chanting or singing beautiful words while holding your water containers. You may also hold a tuning fork on the side of the containers to adjust the frequency of the water. If you are unsure of which tuning fork to use, the OM tuning fork is a good choice.[10]

---

9 The website Blue Bottle Love (www.bluebottlelove.com) has beautiful cobalt-blue glass water containers available for purchase with words such as "Divine Harmony" and "Gratitude" sandblasted on the side.

10 For more information on sound healing, see www.shensounds.com.

- Add a small amount of Himalayan salt to your water pitcher. For example, one pinch for a large pitcher of water would work. Make certain the salt is Himalayan and not iodized or table salt. We encourage you to use your intuition to determine the right amount for your body.

- Place your water container in the full moon to remove negative energies and in direct sunlight to add positive energy and Macroversal wisdom. Even one hour in bright sunlight can add important information to your water. For best results, however, we recommend three full sun/moon cycles, or 72 hours.

Note: Bright sunlight is best for making Harmony Water. If you do not have access to direct sunlight, Himalayan salt lamps will help energize your water.

Photo Credit: Naomi Arnold

You will be amazed at some of the miraculous things you will see when natural sunlight shines directly into your harmonized water. Remember to pay attention because this is how water speaks to you.

Now, you might be wondering, if all water molecules are equally vibrant and healthy, then why is it important to drink purified or harmonized water? Why not just drink out of the tap? The answer is that although all water molecules are equally *capable*, they are not equally energized. So water located near a nuclear power plant has a different energetic imprint than water that comes from a mountain spring untouched by human hands. You must overcome the previous energetic imprinting of water before communicating with water. Thus, if you drink chemically treated water, your body will experience a different level of communication within your cells than if you drink harmonized water. In order to operate at the highest frequencies and to facilitate clear and uninterrupted communication with water, it is imperative that you drink water of the most harmonious vibration.

Ingest Positive Energy

Whether it is the food you eat or the thoughts you entertain, it is imperative that you maintain control over the frequencies you allow into your physical body and your energetic space. Drinking harmonized water is an essential aspect of this process. However, it is also important that you select food that is fresh, organic and free from toxins when possible. Processed foods, genetically modified foods, and foods with chemical additives will serve to lower your vibration while whole, natural, unadulterated, farm-fresh foods will increase your frequency. Likewise, positive words, uplifting music, and loving thoughts will assist your evolutionary development. Some of the uninformative and low-minded entertainment on television can have the opposite effect. Carefully select your television viewing choices. It is also important to choose your thoughts wisely and be careful about the people and the energies you allow into your personal space. Negative thoughts carry with them negative vibrations, while positive thoughts carry higher, more positive vibrations. Similarly, individual human beings carry with them a particular vibration. If you find yourself energetically drained after spending time with a person, take note, because that person's energy field is negatively affecting your personal space. Take responsibility for the people you allow into your life and for the thoughts and emotions you entertain. Make harmony a priority in your daily life.

Add Himalayan Salt

We encourage you to incorporate pure pink Himalayan salt into your diet.[*] In addition to adding a small amount of Himalayan salt to your Harmony Water, we suggest you also add it to the food you eat and even to the surface of your skin. Iodized salt and regular sea salt do *not* perform the same function, so please avoid them if possible. We suggest creating a saltwater mixture to spray on your body by using harmonized water and additional Himalayan salt and adding it to a spray bottle (preferably glass). Spray this on your skin several times throughout the day. Pure Himalayan salt is an important conductor of energy and a purifier of toxins. As it moves through your body, it absorbs and removes denser energies from your body. Therefore, it is of the utmost importance that you release salt water regularly through sweating, perhaps through exercise or steam rooms. Bikram yoga, or yoga performed in a hot room, is a wonderful way to move salt water through your body and to establish resonance with the higher frequencies of water. If such options are not available to you, start by supercharging your daily routine. Add extra energy to your chores, take the stairs, go for longer walks...whatever it takes to work up a sweat and move salt through your body.

Receive Sunlight through Water

We also suggest spending time daily receiving information directly from the sun, for it is the purest source of "news" available to you.

---

[*] Every person is unique. Please consult with your physician before making any changes to your diet.

We strongly recommend you receive this information while you are *immersed in water*. This could mean swimming in the ocean or a pool on a sunny day or using a bathtub or shower where the sun can shine down on you. It is important that light come through water around you and into the water inside your body. This prevents the corruption of information by bodily toxins or emotional baggage and allows you to receive light directly into the intelligence of your body. Most information from the sun does not reach the cells of your body in its purity. This is because the information is often blocked or negatively impacted by your thoughts and emotional state. To bypass these possible obstructions, it is best to receive sunlight while immersed in water.

Copyright 2011 © Blue Bottle Love, www.bluebottlelove.com

The water surrounding your body acts as a perfect conductor, bringing information from the sun directly to the water molecules of the recipient. The water molecules will then communicate what they receive with every cell in your body. You will feel better, think more clearly, and experience a greater sense of optimal bodily functioning. Creative insights will come to you easily, and you will see connections that may have previously evaded your perception.

Integrate Color

Now that you have opened the pathways for communication with water by establishing a resonant frequency within your body, the next step is integrating color to better harmonize your vibration with that of water. Color is integral to the revelation process. Utilizing color appropriately begins with understanding the true nature of color. Color is a dimension of matter and is an important key to unlocking both the macro- and microdimensions existing beyond your current visible spectrum. How would you explain color? You might describe it as a visual attribute or an aesthetic characteristic. However, color also tells a story. Color expresses something about matter—its healing properties and its energetic powers. You could say that color reveals the life purpose of the matter it reflects. For example, much of nature is green: forests, trees, grass, even herbs. Why do you think that is? Green has to do with growth and nurturing, with peace and harmony, stability and constancy. Human skin enjoys only a small range of color expression, and this is representative of the limitation and density of physical life for humans. However, the expression of spirit is far more expansive and varied. Thus, the human aura expresses itself in a rainbow of colors, each representative of a specific life mission. Thus, you might say that the color of an aura tells us a story of the *focus* of that person's life.

Color is an energetic expression of purpose, or intention. Color is experienced as a characteristic of matter or spirit and is readable, transferable, absorbable, communicative and amplifiable. As we said, color has a story to tell, and learning to read color requires an understanding of the various expressions of color and the purpose of each individual color. Color is transferable through the replication of frequency, and this can be achieved on the molecular level or through sound modification. Color can be absorbed in a number of ways: through the eyes or through skin cells, energetically through electromagnetic frequency, by matching resonance among water molecules, through visualization using the sixth chakra, and by directing light through the energetic pathways of the body. Color communicates through a magnetic frequency emitted and replicated by resonant conjoining energies. Color can be amplified through appropriate crystals. For general amplification, we recommend quartz, labradorite, amethyst, and diamonds. Color can also be amplified with sound when combined with exposure. For example, using tuning forks on or around the body while performing color healing can be quite effective. Exposure can mean many things—directed colored light, wearing a color, seeing a color, meditating on a color, sitting in a colored room or under a colored stained glass, anything in which you immerse yourself in a single color at a time.

Saturation, or maximum color absorption, can be achieved by drinking color-energized water, using colorpuncture techniques, or using chromotherapy technology. Water can be easily energized with color. Placing water in a colored glass container in sunlight for a minimum of one hour is a way to do this.

If you do not have colored glass, you can place a colored cloth around a clear glass pitcher or tape colored paper to the sides of the pitcher before placing it in the sun. As you may know, color-puncture is colored light acupuncture, in which colored lights are used on acupuncture points instead of needles. Immersing yourself in color-infused water is also quite effective. This is a form of chromotherapy, a healing technique utilizing color to balance and harmonize the frequencies of the body. In chromotherapy, water within a bath, whirlpool, hot tub, or even swimming pool is energized, allowing for complete immersion within one color or a sequence of colors. This can be done with underwater lights or appropriately used lasers. One of the most effective color-healing techniques involves directed sunlight. Color-enhanced natural sunlight can produce profound results. Rays of light from the sun can be easily enhanced by filtering them through colored sheer cloths over windows or by using crystals, prisms, and colored glass to direct the effects of natural sunlight through specific colors.

Color is a magnificent healing tool. It may interest you to consider the colors most often utilized by modern society—gray, brown, tan, taupe. These colors contain very low electromagnetic frequencies and as such have a neutral or negative effect on the body's magnetic auric fields. Color is used abundantly for children, and you may notice that children have much more energy, joy, playfulness, creativity, and imagination than adults. This is heavily impacted by color exposure. Color can heal, awaken, inspire, attract, release, and renew a person. It is important to learn the healing qualities of individual colors, and we encourage you to move beyond the seven basic colors of the rainbow and into blended colors as well. A slight variation in color can have an enormously different impact on a person.

Color is intricately connected to water. Color therapy works specifically on the water molecules within the human body. Wearing a particular color actually stimulates a targeted response among the water in your body. In fact, color therapy is a necessary tool for unlocking coded information inside your water molecules. To effectively unlock the Water Code inside you, we suggest utilizing the healing properties of colors. We could write an entire book on color healing alone. What we intend here is to provide you with a brief introduction to the healing properties of colors so you can begin tapping into the incredible power of color in preparation to receive the Water Code. If you are interested in incorporating color techniques into a professional healing practice, we would suggest a much more in-depth study of color than what is provided here.

DARK BLUE/BLACK: Similar to the nighttime sky, this color can be useful in opening you to the mysteries of the unknown. It encourages you to take risks, make new discoveries, and think about things in new ways. It can be used to open up dormant pathways in the brain or to unlock information hidden deep within the subconscious. This color should be used only on targeted areas of the body and not for immersion. Specifically, we recommend using directed light or placing colored cloths or coordinating crystals on the inside of the wrists, top of the spine, top of the head (crown chakra), and bottom of the feet. Recommended stones for amplification include obsidian, onyx, black tourmaline, and black sapphire.

ROYAL BLUE: Blue works to transition you into the higher chakras similar to an energetic corridor. It also creates a space for quantum exploration. Blue stimulates the water inside the physical body, bringing the body into open communication with all parts of itself. Blue is useful on the throat chakra and the third eye, for these are both doorways to communication. For an immediate effect, focus blue light on the back of the head near the location of the pineal gland or at the top of the spine. Coordinating stones such as sapphire, sodalite, blue kyanite, and tanzanite, may also be used.

TURQUOISE: This color provides inspiration, encourages growth, facilitates the opening of communication channels and assists in accessing the universal mind. You can use turquoise to pull your essence into the physical or to connect with your divine self while in physical form. It is ideally used only around the head and shoulders and is often focused on the forehead. It is stimulating in a safe and gentle way. To amplify turquoise in targeted areas, use stones such as chrysocolla, turquoise, labradorite, and dioptase.

LIGHT BLUE: A soothing color, light blue is useful in coun-teracting stress, aggravation, and negative feelings associated with self-criticism. Light blue provides a sense of calm, safety, security, and self-confidence. Light blue is the color of the sky, and as such, it shields the planet with the intention of soothing, calming and gently empowering its inhabitants. Light blue is effective when used over the entire body to envelop the body in a cool, loving, and protective vibration. This color can also be used on the third eye to remove doubt and promote acceptance of what is. Recommended stones include angelite, celestite, blue lace agate, blue aventurine, and blue quartz.

EMERALD GREEN: This is the color of light transformed into material energy. Emerald green is an empowering color, promoting optimal health, well-being, and commu-nity. Green is a color of rejuvenation and growth. Green light or green cloths can be used on the lower and middle chakras. Stones such as moldavite, malachite, green agate, emerald, and chrysoprase also amplify the energy of this color. Because of its vibration of growth, green should not be used on tumors, cancer, or similar ailments.

LIGHT GREEN: Growth through enlightenment is the inten-tion of this color. Light green is excellent for issues relating to the blood, circulation, and life force energy. It assists with hair growth and can be used over the entire body for its regenerative effects. It assists with the production of new cells. It is also a color that promotes youthfulness and guards against aging. The healing properties of this color may be amplified through colored light, clothing, or stones such as green apophyllite, green aventurine, and green calcite.

GOLD: Gold is a stimulating color that refines the frequen-cies of mineral elements in your body. It assists with the deficiencies of vitamins and minerals and is excellent for boosting the functioning of the immune system. Gold light provides a protective shield around the physical body and is highly recommended for those undergoing medical procedures. It provides strength, stamina, and power for the physical, mental, and emotional bodies. Gold light or cloth is excellent when used over the entire body and can also be used to infuse extra strength through the feet, hands, and spine. Suggested stones include pyrite, gold, citrine, and tiger's eye.

YELLOW: Yellow represents light energy and thus works well as a complement to any other color. Yellow encourages alertness, concentration, and playfulness. Yellow communicates with the light within cells, awakening the pathways of the nervous system and increasing the responsiveness of the entire physical body. Yellow promotes a positive attitude, self-confidence, appreciation, and gratitude. Yellow can be used over the entire body but is most effective when focused on the spine, the head, and the face. Coordinating stones include calcite, golden beryl, yellow sapphire, and yellow tourmaline.

PEACH: Peach is a color of comfort, harmony, and creativity. Peach is uplifting and inspirational. Peach encourages cohesion and unity, often successfully bringing the physical, mental, emotional, and spiritual bodies into alignment. It is a great color for balancing and is useful when peach light is directed to one half of the body at a time at equal and coordinated intervals. Peach-colored clothing and Himalayan salt lamps amplify the energy of this color.

ORANGE: This color is very effective in mitigating headaches, muscle pain, and joint tenderness. Orange stimulates creative action and increases energy throughout the body. Orange can be used to treat broken bones, depression, and blood loss. It regulates the flow of energy throughout the body, adding it or reducing it where needed. Orange assists with concentration, focus, and the removal of negative vibrations within the body and its energy fields. Orange is best used all over the body but is also useful when directed to any of the chakras. Orange light or cloths or stones such as carnelian, orange calcite, fire agate, or orange jade can be used to amplify this color.

RED: Red is a stimulating and agitating color that produces intense and immediate results within the body and aura. Red is not recommended for use over the entire body, but it can be quite effective when directed toward particular areas. Red can be excellent for skin conditions such as acne or discoloration. Red is useful for increasing energy and responsiveness, especially for conditions such as a coma, trauma, and energetic blockage. Red light is useful directed in small amounts to elbows, knees, ankles, the inner wrists, and the temples. Coordinating stones such as garnet, jasper, ruby, red carnelian, and red tourmaline may be used. Representing the element of fire, red must be balanced with an increased intake of water into and over the body. Red is also useful in facilitating past life memories and accessing suppressed childhood trauma.

PINK: Reminiscent of the primordial ocean and our birth into individual consciousness, pink is a dearly beloved color, providing nourishment to the spirit and energetic fields of the body. Pink is a highly charged color with very subtle energy. It is used extensively in healing because it is energized with the vibration of love, the most powerful energy in the universe. Pink encourages self- love, harmonious interactions, awareness, and loving thoughts. Pink light, clothing, and coordinating stones such as rose quartz, kunzite, morganite, pink carnelian, and rhodonite are recommended. Pink can be used on any part of the body or on the entire body. This color cannot be overused, as the ability to give and receive love is infinite.

MAGENTA: Magenta is wonderful for cardiovascular health and for healing the overused portions of the mind. Magenta is an amplifier of like energy and is able to move energy through the veins, through the segments of the human brain, and through the emotional dimensions of the human experience. Magenta is effective when utilized on pressure points and energy centers, skillfully clearing blockages and balancing energy outflow and inflow. Suggested stones include magenta fluorite, pink agate and magenta sapphire. We recommend magenta light and magenta clothing to enhance the effects of this color. Magenta is helpful when used in conjunction with past-life or between-life regressions. It is also useful in amplifying your highest path.

VIOLET: Violet is a color of ease and the beautiful unfolding of spiritual evolution. It is the color of synchronicity and blending at the highest levels. It is a wonderful color for psychic protection and is especially helpful for infants and children. Violet would be an excellent color choice for a nursery. Violet is a color of spiritual knowing and remembrance. It is effective for targeted healing of the throat, third eye and crown chakras, and for all-over healing. Recommended stones include violet amethyst, sugilite, lavender jade, and lepidolite. Violet is Macroversally known as the color representing the highest good of All That Is.

PURPLE: Purple is the color of the underworld and is very useful in stimulating the imagination to break through the boundaries of your reality. Purple represents the mysteries of the quantum realms and is an excellent conductor of higher frequencies. Wearing purple transfers the power of the unseen realms to the wearer. Purple can be used to stimulate the kidneys, the heart center, and the pineal gland. Directed light and coordinating stones such as charoite, purple fluorite, and purple tourmaline may be used on the wrists, ankles, and other joints.

<u>INDIGO:</u> Indigo is a sacred color of ancient importance that is very effective in interdimensional bridging and extradimensional communication. Indigo is widely known as the color of reunion and resonance. Because of its intensity, it is not recommended for all-over healing. Indigo is best used for targeted areas such as the throat chakra, third-eye chakra, or, ideally, the crown chakra. It can be used on the inside of the palms and the inside of the heels. Recommended stones include lapis lazuli, azurite, and iolite. Water that has been energized with the color indigo can be useful in treating aggressive diseases such as cancer, Parkinson's, AIDS, and rheumatoid arthritis. Wearing indigo jewelry is recommended for stimulating your vision beyond the physical world and for initiating extradimensional communication.

Color Sequences

Color sequences are another method of utilizing color to bring about important vibratory shifts in your physical, mental, emotional, and energetic bodies so that you may easily and effortlessly unlock the Water Code inside of you. Color sequences are patterns of color arranged in a particular order and ratio. This can be accomplished by using colored cloths or sheets of colored paper, one after another in the appropriate sequence. This can also be done on your computer by meditating on one colored screen and then another. Websites such as www.mindbodyhealing.com offer color sequence therapy for a fee. You have the option for creating your own color sequence on this website. Remember, you can increase the time for each sequence as long as the appropriate ratios are maintained.

<u>RELEASING BLOCKAGES</u>

Orange (10 seconds)
Gold (10 seconds)

Red (5 seconds)
Pink (15 seconds)

GAINING FOCUS

Violet (5 seconds)
Magenta (5 seconds)
Indigo (15 seconds)

GROWTH

Light grass green (10 seconds)
Emerald green (15 seconds)
Sapphire blue (10 seconds)

ENERGETIC CLEANSING

Purple (5 seconds)
Orange (10 seconds)
Violet (10 seconds)
Gold (15 seconds)

Additional Suggestions for Raising Your Vibration

As scientists from quite far in the future, we offer you the following guidance for preparing your body to receive water's message. Here are some of our suggestions for raising your vibratory frequency to establish resonance with water:

- Drink much more water than you currently do. We would double the recommended dose currently provided by health practitioners. You will eliminate toxins faster and speed up your natural evolutionary progress.

- Learn from nature. Nature has a story. Its origins are as ancient as Earth herself. Remember who your true teachers are. Much information is available to you, but you must know where to look. Begin by listening to nature. Spend as much time as possible in quiet solitude in a beautiful outside setting.

- Know that the next great frontier in scientific discovery lies in the quantum dimensions but that these dimensions are not accessible with your current scientific methodology. Understanding these dimensions means understanding the richness of multidimensionality. A one-dimensional approach will not even scratch the surface of what lies within.

- Begin integrating your understanding of the unseen into your daily life. This involves the power of manifestation, the laws of energy, and the significance of nonmatter. Be a pioneer of this in your daily life. Prioritize your energetic focus and intention because this is the key to manifestation in the physical realm. Lead others by example in your understanding and implementation of this in your own life.

- Retrain your body using musical harmonics and vibrational frequency. This can be achieved by using tuning forks on your body or listening to uplifting frequencies such as 528 Hz, the frequency of love.[11] These are keys to maintaining a youthful appearance, longevity, and vibrant health. Start by making this a daily practice. This will produce great results rather quickly.

---

11   This frequency, 528 Hz, is known as the "frequency of love," or the "DNA repair frequency." Samples are available on websites such as YouTube or iTunes.

- Understand the concept of fuel for your body. Fuel comes in the form of food, thought, emotion, and environmental exposure. Ingesting improper fuel is like using gasoline to power an electric car. You cannot expect a body to thrive that has not been given proper fuel.

- Begin to understand and implement color therapy for emotional, physical, mental, and spiritual health and longevity. What you will discover as you continue down this path is that the future of science is intricately linked to color therapy. In our realms, we refer to this as Color Integration and Healing.

- Stop the cycle of death and quit ingesting the vibration of death into your body. It is energetically inconsistent with life and longevity and is detrimental to your health and well-being. Select fuel that is alive and know that you are moving into a future where food will not be necessary for the experience of life. You will be able to survive quite comfortably on light and water alone.

- Remember that we are all interconnected. Know what this means on a scientific level—that every action and thought is energetically connected and affects every being experiencing life. Begin to accept social responsibility for your personal experience.

- Take time to recharge yourself by laying on the surface of the Earth and receiving energy from her. You will be surprised at the enormous benefits you will receive from this practice.

- Recognize the incredible significance of the words you speak and the enormous impact they have on your experience of reality.

- Understand that the brain is subdivided into segments and that each segment is responsive to a particular color. Exposure to a particular color can heal and energize the brain and trigger unused portions of it.

- Gain awareness of the significance of moving water through the body through exercise, submersion in water, heat, conscious intention, and ingestion of water by mouth. As you know, water is the great communicator, and as such, it plays a very significant role in internal communication.

5

THE 13-CHAKRA
CENTRAL ENERGY SYSTEM

When all of the chakras are understood,
opened, and connected together,
we have then bridged the gulf between matter
and spirit, understanding that
we, ourselves, are the Rainbow Bridge.[12]

O nce you have achieved resonance with the higher frequencies of water, it is important that the lines of communication in and around your body are open and balanced so that you may receive the Water Code that is revealed to you. This involves understanding and harmonizing the chakra energy centers in your human body. Presently, only seven chakras are widely recognized, but this will soon change. We are honored to share the 13-Chakra Central Energy System with you now.

---

12 Anodea Judith, *Wheels of Life* 2nd ed. (Woodbury, MN: Llewellyn Publications, 2007), 7.

The 13 chakras represent the Central Energy System of the human body. The chakras exist along the midline of the human body, extending from just below your feet to the crown of your head. The 13 chakras constitute the primary points of energy output and input for the human body. In Western culture, the term "chakra" has been interpreted to mean "energy center." However, this is not entirely accurate. Chakras *are* energy centers in the body but not all energy centers are chakras. Consider the practice of acupuncture. This ancient form of Chinese medicine recognizes over 2,000 energy points in the human body. These energy points identify important places where energy meridians can be accessed. However, the chakra system represents the 13 major energy centers of the body where energy flows in and out in cone-shaped or vortex-like patterns. The 13 chakras comprising the Central Energy System of the human body are:

13 – Crown
12 – All-Seeing Eye or Third Eye
11 – Harmony
10 – Sound or Throat
9 – Breath or Thymus
8 – Heart
7 – Solar Plexus
6 – Creation
5 – Manifestation or Portal
4 – Grounding Cord
3 – Altar
2 – Base
1 – Boundary

THE 13-CHAKRA CENTRAL ENERGY SYSTEM

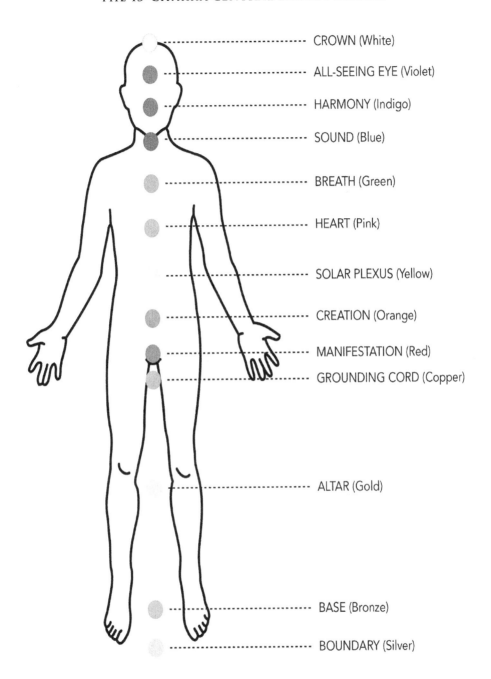

CROWN (White)

ALL-SEEING EYE (Violet)

HARMONY (Indigo)

SOUND (Blue)

BREATH (Green)

HEART (Pink)

SOLAR PLEXUS (Yellow)

CREATION (Orange)

MANIFESTATION (Red)

GROUNDING CORD (Copper)

ALTAR (Gold)

BASE (Bronze)

BOUNDARY (Silver)

Auric Energy Fields

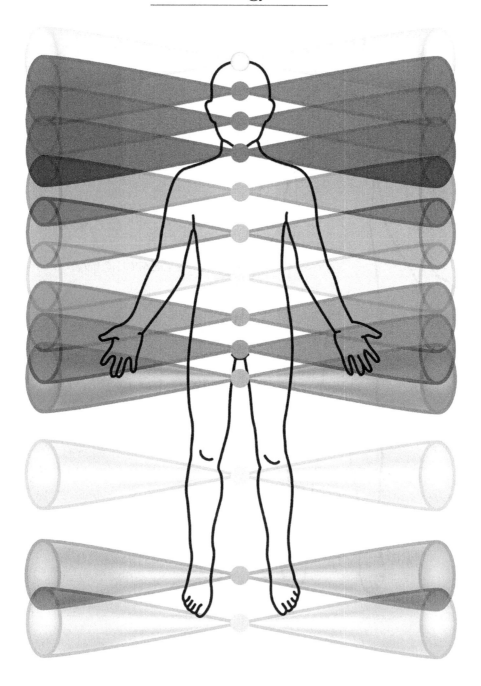

Each chakra creates a cone-shaped energy field extending outward from it. On paper, it may look like two outward pointing cones meeting in the center at a point. However, it is helpful to think of the cones as energetic vortices. When two spiraling cones of energy meet at a central point and move outward as vortices, they form a tube of energy, almost like a fountain, creating a "torus."

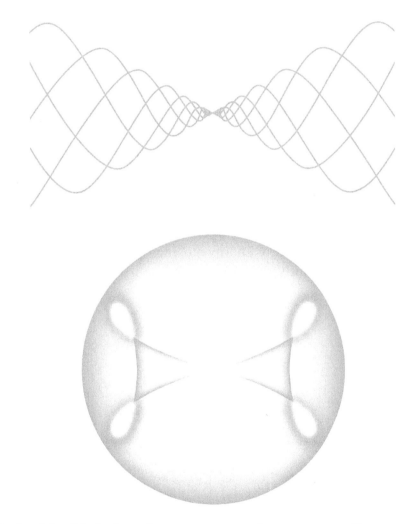

Each of the 13 chakras forms an energetic torus extending outward around the human body. Here is an example of the energy torus created by the heart chakra alone:

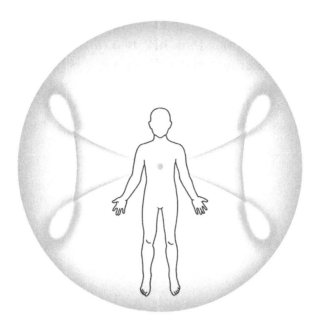

Together, the 13 chakras form an interlocking bubble of energy around the body. In addition to the individual torus-shaped vortices generated by each chakra, the 13 energy centers work together to form one powerful pillar of energy moving up and down the center line of the human body.

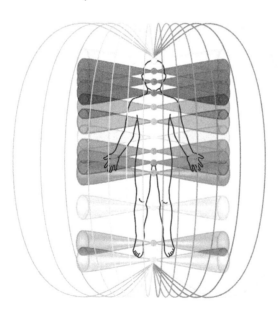

This chakra energy combines to form a single, dynamic, rainbow-colored auric energy field around the body. This is your energetic aura. It is multidimensional, multifaceted, and filled with sacred geometric patterns.

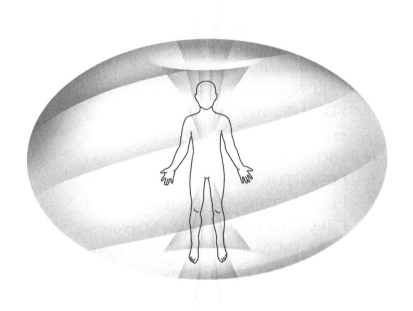

13 Chakra Intentions

The human chakra system is important to understand for three reasons: (1) it helps you relate more effectively with the world around you because by understanding yourself, you understand everything else, (2) it allows you to gain greater awareness of the world beyond your five basic senses, and (3) it assists you in communicating more effectively with the water within your physical body. Once you understand the central energy centers and their functions, you will understand how they correspond with appropriate energetic intentions.

To regard your chakras as intentions is helpful for remembering that each energy center has a *purpose*. By focusing your attention on the 13 Chakra Intentions, you will awaken to the meaning of each Chakra and ultimately to the purpose of the chakra system itself. The 13 Chakra Intentions are:

13 – I AM eternal.
12 – I SEE beyond my physical reality.
11 – I HARMONIZE with the symphony of existence.
10 – I SOUND my signature vibration.
9 – I BREATHE the air of life.
8 – I LOVE all life with compassion.
7 – I RECEIVE the light of the Macroverse.
6 – I CREATE beautiful patterns of light.
5 – I MANIFEST my creations.
4 – I CONNECT to the energy of the universe.
3 – I RESPECT my connection to the galaxy.
2 – I SUPPORT the well-being of the Earth.
1 – I PROTECT the expression of my being.

The Lower Chakras

Before we delve into the individual chakras, we would like to discuss the lower four chakras in general. There has been a misconception that the energy centers below the root chakra represent baser or lower frequencies that humans must rise above.

This thinking is closely associated with the idea of original sin and humans being born "bad"—that is, the roots of the human body are dark, negative, and something humans must save themselves from. It is no surprise that humans have virtually erased the existence of the lower four chakras from the collective consciousness.

You will notice that chakras 1 through 4 are associated with metals of the Earth: silver, bronze, gold and copper. These metals each represent aspects of humanity's relationship to the universe. Silver represents humanity's connection to the moon and of course, to one of the original elements of creation - water. Bronze represents humanity's connection to Earth and the soil out of which life grows. Gold represents humanity's connection to the sun as well as to fire, one of the original elements of creation. Copper is liquid energy and represents humanity's connection to light, the life force of All That Is.

It is quite interesting that knowledge of these chakras and the special significance of their associated metals have been lost by humanity. Metals are extremely important for connecting human beings to their roots and also for transmitting and receiving information to and from Earth. It is significant to note that the metals of the Earth hold the memory of the planet's life experience, including ancient secrets and the wisdom of the masters who once lived on this planet. It is no coincidence that the loss of conscious memory of the lower chakras coincides with the loss of ancient wisdom and history held by the Earth herself. As you reconnect with the truth of who you are and where you come from, you will also find a revival of your connection to the sacred metals that make up the fundamental structure upon which the human body functions. Bringing the properties of these metals into human consciousness will have vast and far-reaching effects on all life.

1st Chakra
BOUNDARY CHAKRA
SILVER

"I PROTECT"

Moon ✦ Water ✦ Magnetism ✦ "Liquid Mercury"

This chakra is located just below the base of your feet. The boundary chakra is associated with the metal silver. Silver creates a highly charged energetic shield around the outer edge of your aura, forming a shell of protection from disharmonious energies. This chakra is an important source of protective energy for the human body, representing the distinction between a body's personal energy and the energy of the collective and noncollective realities. The 1st chakra forms a magnetic boundary around the body with its electromagnetic frequency and magnetic properties. Magnets can attract or repel depending on proximity, resonant frequency, and corresponding quantum properties. Because the boundary chakra is electromagnetic, it carries with it highly charged magnetic particles. It is the outer boundary of the human energy field and is intended to provide energetic protection to the human form.

Silver is a sacred metal and has long been associated with special protective powers. Silver is connected to the 1st chakra in large part because of this chakra's highly charged energetic composition and its position relative to the rest of the human body. There is a strong association between the 1st chakra and the moon. We invite you to consider the role the moon plays in relation to the Earth. Where did the moon come from? How does the moon look compared to the sun and to Earth? Could the moon have been built by an ancient civilization, and if so, why would they have built it? What purpose does the moon serve? What purpose does the boundary chakra serve the human body? Ah, it is so much fun to learn and to remember, now, isn't it?

When you observe the human experience on Planet Earth, what do you see? Probably the first thing you notice is a problem with freedom and personal space. Everyone seems to be stepping on everyone else's personal space, and individuals do not seem to have adequate protection or boundaries. Why is this? Well, one reason for this situation is a disconnection from and lack of awareness of the 1st chakra—the boundary chakra. Humans can help to transform the Freedom dilemma on Earth by focusing on their 1st chakras. You can do this by energizing the outer boundary of your energy field with luminous silver light and appropriate corresponding stones and metals such as hematite, silver, platinum, lead, aluminum, and magnetite. Moonstone, galena, or any feldspar crystal would also work. Some people like to visualize a protective hematite bubble around their energy field. An even more effective technique, however, is to put a liquid mercury boundary, or bubble, around your personal energy field. Mercury, or quicksilver, also has strong associations with the 1st chakra. Mercury is not yet fully understood by humans at this point in time. However, mercury is very active in the quantum realms and acts as a powerful bridge between the Macroverse and the Microverse. Now say to yourself:

"I PROTECT
the expression of my being
by energizing my boundary chakra
with a bubble of liquid mercury.
I AM PROTECTED."

2nd Chakra
BASE CHAKRA
BRONZE

"I SUPPORT"

Earth ✦ Soil ✦ The Feet ✦ "Liquid Earth"

The base chakra is located in the center of the feet and acts to support the human body. The base chakra is sometimes referred to as "liquid Earth" because it blends the human aura with the soil of the planet. If you envision the human body as a tree, the feet would become like the soil of the Earth, representing the ground out of which the human body grows. The feet support the weight of the human body just as the Earth supports the weight of life living on the planet. Like good planting soil, the 2nd chakra allows the human energy field to take hold and spread its roots into the ground of the Earth. The base chakra blends its energy with the planet, allowing Earth's energy to move up into the human body while also encouraging the root energy fields of the human aura to dig deep into the Earth herself.

Consider humanity's relationship to Mother Earth. Humans show very little respect for the life she gives and the wisdom she provides. This has resulted in a great divide between humans and the planet. In truth, this predicament is a reflection of the disconnect between humans and their base chakras. The initial step toward manifesting a harmonious future for humans and Planet Earth is to begin recognizing and energizing the 2nd chakra—the base chakra. It is also important to develop a connection with the metal bronze by adding it to your home, by wearing it, and by spending time touching it and holding it. Bronze is a metal of strength, providing structure and support to the energetic bodies of human beings. Bronze holds form quite well and is long lasting. It is no coincidence that your own civilization has used bronze to preserve baby shoes. It has been used by many ancient civilizations to create statues and statutory bases for works of art and other historic records.

Bronze light can be used to repair the 2nd chakra and so can strategically placed bronze or iron metals. Also effective are corresponding stones such as tiger's eye, brown agate, bronzite, and smoky quartz. To energize your base chakra, imagine a bronze bubble of energy just inside your silver boundary chakra, originating from the center point of your feet. Say to yourself:

"I SUPPORT
the well-being of the Earth
by energizing my base chakra
with a bubble of bronze Earth energy.
I AM SUPPORTED."

3rd Chakra
ALTAR CHAKRA
GOLD

"I RESPECT"

Sun ✦ Fire ✦ Skeletal System ✦ "The Golden Altar"

The 3rd chakra has been called "the golden altar" and is one of the most sacred energy centers of the human body. You will remember that an altar is a raised structure on which offerings and sacrifices are made to the divine. Correspondingly, the 3rd chakra is located at an elevated point in the human body, situated in the area between the knees. An altar also represents an awareness or recognition of your place in relation to All That Is. This chakra's function is not about religion or worship but about a greater perspective that includes respect for that which cannot be seen as well as that which can be seen with the eyes. The location of this chakra is notable because kneeling and prayer are so often associated with each other.

The 3rd chakra is an important meeting place for the natural and the divine. It is the core of the physical body or the bones that form the frame upon which the body is built. Upon this structure the ultimate sacrifice of bringing spirit into physical form is made. The very act of incarnation demonstrates a respect for the intricacy of creation and the expression of life itself. The associated metal for the altar chakra is gold. Gold is known for its alchemical properties and its divine origins. Gold carries with it the energies of the sun and fire, a building block of the universe. Gold is sacred, as is life itself. There are many reasons you will find golden altars throughout the religious history of the Earth. In mythology, gold is a material of the gods that has been shared with humans. In fact, it should not be surprising to learn that gold has extraterrestrial origins, which is why it is revered for its specialness among "ordinary" metals.

Something you may have noticed is a minimal degree of contact with other life in the galaxy. In theory, in a Universe of Space and Time, Earth should have a relationship with nearby planetary and star-based life. Why has this contact not happened for the majority of humans? Many of you believe that your governments have conspired to prevent this relationship. To some extent, this is true. However, if Earth is one of the most primitive, if not *the* most primitive planet in the galaxy, does it not seem logical that such contact could not be prevented by an Earth-based government? If Earth's galactic neighbors are more advanced technologically and evolutionarily, wouldn't you expect some sort of direct physical contact with them? The reason for this separation is simple. Many humans lack respect for their place in the galaxy and for their galactic neighbors. This lack of respect is both conscious and unconscious and is a reflection of humanity's separation from the 3rd chakra—the altar chakra.

To develop a connection with the altar chakra, it is helpful to understand the meaning of the "golden altar." In ancient times (prehistory), people of Earth created meeting places for civilizations to experience physical connections with other life in the galaxy. Often, Earth civilizations did not have the means to physically travel to other locations in the galaxy, so people created golden altars as signposts for extraterrestrial civilizations. Gold is a metal widely recognized and utilized by civilizations throughout the galaxy, so it was a natural choice for these meeting places. Gold is also rare and a bit difficult to possess on Planet Earth, so these locations would be quite clear and easy to locate for outside visitors. Now, over the past few thousand years, altars have lost their meaning and have essentially become artifacts of an ancient time. This is a reflection of humanity's disconnection from the 3rd chakra and from other life in the galaxy.

To restore this energy field and begin reconnecting with Earth's galactic neighbors requires a reunion with the substance of gold. If gold is not easily had, golden stones such as pyrite and chalcopyrite also work. Now imagine a bubble of shiny gold energy just inside your base chakra emanating from the energy center located between your knees. Say to yourself:

"I RESPECT
my connection to the galaxy
by energizing my altar chakra
with a bubble of golden galactic energy.
I AM RESPECTED."

4th Chakra
GROUNDING CORD CHAKRA
COPPER

"I CONNECT"

Light ✦ Spine ✦ Nervous System ✦ "Liquid Energy"

The grounding cord is the 4th chakra and is associated with the metal copper. The 4th chakra has great connective powers because of its ability to connect with and utilize light energy. This is your electrical circuit. It "plugs you in" to the Earth's electrical field and the energy field in the center of the universe. The grounding cord conducts information via electromagnetic frequency.

Many have recognized the existence of the grounding cord but have not yet associated it with a specific chakra in the human body. The grounding cord is closely related to the body's nervous system, acting as an energy highway that connects human beings to the center of the Earth and to the center of the universe. Copper activates all of the energy centers in the human body and is the key to proper functioning of the body's energetic field. Copper is a very strong conductor of energy and is highly useful in interpersonal, interspecies, and interdimensional communication. We recommend that you wear copper whenever you intend to connect with the outer or inner realms.

You have probably noticed that humans have an energy problem. Most people lack energy and feel tired, separated, and alone. This is not because you are alone! This is because humans have lost their connection to their energy source. The energy source exists as a balance between three areas: the Earth, the spine, and the center of the universe. If you imagine your spine as a copper cord with plugs on both ends and electrical sockets in the center of the universe and the center of Earth, you can imagine that humans have been walking around "unplugged."

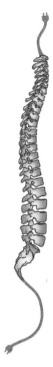

It is time to plug back in! Start by imagining your spinal cord filled with bright, expansive copper energy. Now, see the cord inside of this copper energy expanding down into the center of the Earth until it reaches the source of Earth energy. Plug the copper cord in and feel the electricity shooting up the cord into your spine. Now imagine the copper cord coming out of the top of your spine and reaching into space all the way to the center of the universe. Plug in to the center of the universe's energy. See the electrical copper energy lighting up your entire cord and filling your spine with radiant rainbow light. It is important that the 4th chakra stay open and connected so the physical body remains plugged in to the wisdom of the Earth and the energy of the universe.

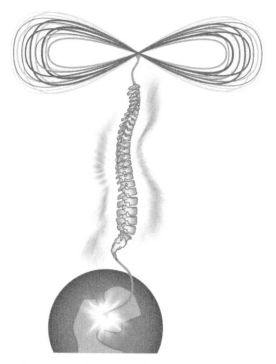

To fully utilize the grounding cord, it is helpful to imagine copper energy moving up and down your spine and into your brain. Fill your spine with copper energy and then visualize a copper cord connecting you down into the center of the Earth and all the way up into the center of the universe. When activating the 4th chakra, it is best to always use copper metal, although carnelian can also be used to amplify the copper energy. As you do this, say to yourself:

"I CONNECT
to the energy of the universe
by plugging my copper grounding cord
into the center of the Earth and the
heart of the universe.
I AM CONNECTED."

Remembering and reenergizing these lower four chakras and the metals of the Earth associated with them is an important step in humanity's evolution. Once these roots are established, the upper nine chakras will work much more efficiently and effectively. Let us progress through the upper chakras.

The Upper Chakras

5th Chakra
MANIFESTATION CHAKRA
RED

"I MANIFEST"

Portal ✦ Birth Canal ✦ Menstruation ✦ Salt ✦ Sexual Organs ✦ "Doorway to Life"

The 5th chakra is the manifestation or portal chakra and represents the doorway between the Microverse and the Macroverse. This threshold between worlds is a very sacred place holding large amounts of intense energy. The 5th chakra is situated in the lowermost part of the human torso and is associated with the human genitalia. The manifestation chakra is where your creations are manifested and shared with the world. It is also this same energy center that houses the birth canal and allows new life to emerge into the Earth experience. The ability to create new life is a fundamental attribute of divine power. The energy of this chakra has been underutilized, misinterpreted, and exploited. Thus, its connection to divine power has been lost. The modern view of this as the root chakra is not accurate, for your roots extend from your feet. Most likely, this chakra has been confused with the grounding cord chakra.

The 5th chakra is the portal of entry into the physical world. From this chakra new life is born and creative ideas are made manifest in the world. The manifestation chakra is the seat of power for human beings; the place where kundalini energy is thought to reside. Sexual expression is associated with the 5th chakra and is often misdirected and highly misunderstood. Sexual deviance and dysfunction are typically connected to the repression of creative manifestation in both men and women. The manifestation of creative expression is important for everyone but is absolutely essential for men as well as for women who do not give birth. Childbirth is one way to release 5th chakra energy, although there are many ways to bring a creation into form.

The manifestation chakra is a portal through which energy from the inside moves outside and vice versa. It is a passageway where waste leaves the body and where new life enters the world. Although human waste can be a very distasteful thing, it also represents the transformation of by-products into new life. You are on the forefront of discovering the many uses of human waste as renewable energy, so try to separate from your innate disdain for it. This same energy center also sees the release of menstrual blood from inside the body. This monthly flow connects women to the flow of the lifeblood of the planet—the oceans. Both are the by-product of creation and both contain an essential element for creative manifestation—salt. It is very important to utilize the vibrational signature of salt for any creative manifestation. Many people drink sole regularly[13] or use Himalayan salt crystal lamps to energize their creative space. The importance of integrating the ancient salt vibration cannot be emphasized enough.

The manifestation chakra is associated with the color red and is best energized with targeted glowing red light or red stones such as ruby, garnet, and bloodstone. As you imagine ruby red glowing energy moving out of your 5th chakra in vortex-like cones and forming a bubble of glowing red energy around you, say to yourself:

---

13   Barbara Hendel and Peter Ferreira, "The Sole" in *Water & Salt: The Essence of Life* (N.p: Natural Resources, 2003), 144-59.

**"I MANIFEST
my creativity
by energizing my portal chakra
with the glowing red light of creation.
I MANIFEST MY CREATIONS."**

6th Chakra
CREATION CHAKRA
ORANGE

"I CREATE"

Sacred Geometry ✦ Patterns of Light ✦ Womb ✦ Formation ✦
"Womb of Creation"

The creation chakra is the 6th chakra, the place where creative ideas come together and form. It is a place of nurturing and feeding. It is the womb of life. In the human body, it is associated with a mother's womb, not to be confused with the sexual organs. It is located just above the pubic bone and is affiliated with the color orange.

The 6th chakra is the birthplace of creation, the place where new form is nurtured and the place where the soul enters the body for the first time. When an essence decides to have a life experience inside of a particular body, it sends its soul into the body during formation. A soul can technically enter a body from the moment of conception up until the moment of birth. The time of entry varies for everybody and depends on an array of matters personal to the individual soul. Some mothers have a close enough connection to the entering soul that they will know the moment the soul arrives. Others may have the experience of birthing a brand new soul or a soul they have never met before, and this may result in a more

73

distant feeling. In any case, the soul will enter into the fetus of its chosen human body through the creation chakra, located below the lower abdomen, where the womb exists.

A common question among humans is why the creation of life occurs only inside the female body. You will, of course, notice this is also true of most animals. Many people wonder if men have the same chakras as women since men do not have a womb. The answer is yes, all humans have the same energy centers, although they are not equally active and utilized. In men, the 6th chakra is typically underutilized. For both men and women, the 6th chakra is the source of creative germination. This is where new ideas are born. Men who are highly creative tend to have a very well-developed 6th chakra. The 6th chakra in women is inherently more active due to the possibility of new life and the existence of the womb. This is why it is *typically* easier for women to engage in creative activities and why such activity feels much more natural for them.

Creation represents a merging of energies. In the creation of human life, a sperm and an egg join in harmonious interrelationship. In reference to a creative idea, the 6th chakra is where the creative idea is birthed. When you think about unformed creative energy, what is that? You may consider it light without form. Thus, in the act of creation, this unformed light comes together with focus and intention, in harmonious relationship, to form beautiful patterns. In fact, the basis of all creation lies in sacred geometric patterns of light, which is why you are so drawn to sacred geometry. Every pattern represents a creation of some sort. So when you look at sacred geometric forms, consider what creation is revealed by each pattern. Creation is not necessarily associated with language and certainly not with a particular language, such as English. So how would you communicate or explain a certain creation without language? Most likely with images. Patterns of light.

When you examine crop circles, do you know what they are? They are attempts at communication with the human race in a more universal language of symbols. Some researchers are working through interpretations of crop circles, but most people do not pay attention to them or fear them because they do not understand the patterns with their conscious minds. Creators of crop circles began communicating concepts that should be common knowledge with the intention of creating a channel of intelligent exchange. If you look back through crop circles by date of discovery, discarding those that feel man-made or that do not have a high vibration, you will be able to piece together a message. Once your creation chakra is energized, it will be much easier to connect with your galactic community and better appreciate these patterns of light. Understanding sacred geometry will assist you with the process of creation and will help you relate to the beautiful creative energy all around you. A helpful way to energize your 6th chakra is with geometric patterns of light.

The color of creation is orange and is activated by localized orange light and crystals such as amber, citrine, and orange topaz. To aid the formulation of creative ideas, utilize orange or shades of orange such as peach. Start by imagining cones of orange creative energy coming out of your 6th chakra. You can imagine this light forming beautiful patterns, almost like a kaleidoscope. See these sacred geometric patterns forming around you as you say to yourself:

"I CREATE
beautiful patterns of light
by energizing my creation chakra
with geometric patterns of glowing orange light.
I AM CREATIVE."

7th Chakra
SOLAR PLEXUS CHAKRA
YELLOW

"I RECEIVE"

Reception ✦ Filtration ✦ Water ✦ Urinary System ✦
Light Energy In ✦ "Energy Filter"

Your 7th chakra is what is widely referred to as the solar plexus chakra. The solar plexus chakra is important because this is where you receive information from the world around you. This is where light comes into your body in the form of information. Most people on the planet keep this area wide open and use no filter whatsoever, so they suffer from a great deal of stress and sickness. It is very important that you filter all energy that enters at this chakra so that your energy body is not overwhelmed by the lower vibrations dominating the Earth plane at this moment in time.

The solar plexus chakra is associated with reception and filtration of light energy into the body. It is connected to the urinary system and vibrates to the color yellow. The urinary system has a mechanism for removing unwanted light energy from the body via water. The intricacies and depth of the human urinary system are not really understood at this time. However, this system is quite fascinating. Think about the color of urine. When you are healthy, it is bright or light yellow. When you are unhealthy, it is dark yellow. Your urine can tell you a lot about the type of information going into and out of your body. Is it toxic? How toxic is it? How much is your body having to work to expel it? There is a whole science of urine reading that will soon be discovered by humans. In fact, urine can reveal more about a body's internal health than blood.

There is a lot of unwanted energy floating around in your collective reality. As Lightworkers, you have come to Earth to assist with grounding higher vibrational energy into a lower vibrational reality. That is why it is *absolutely essential* that you develop resonance with your 7th chakra. When people talk about shielding themselves, they are usually referring to shielding their solar plexus from the influx of energy at this point. We understand there are differing opinions on whether it is necessary to shield yourself. Some say it is very important and some say that you should focus on positive light energy or on what you wish to attract rather than what you want to repel. We would say the truth lies somewhere in between. In theory the idea of only focusing on what you wish to attract is correct, for like energy attracts like energy. However, in order to effectively create or exude the positive energy you wish to attract, you must have a clean space, energetically, in which to do so. Given the collective reality you are experiencing, this clean space is not easily had and requires an almost constant state of cleansing and purifying. We are sorry to report this. We wish it were not so. However, you are living in an energetically polluted environment. Thus, it is of the utmost importance that you cleanse and purify your Solar Plexus Chakra regularly so that you are able to manifest the positive reality you wish to attract. Is it enough to say affirmations? Is it enough to visualize what you want? No. As Lightworkers, you must maintain a constant state of cleansing and purifying *in addition* to all of the affirmations, visualizations, positive thinking, and so on.

The best way to cleanse and purify your 7th chakra is by drinking water. The more purified, energized, and harmonized water you can drink, the better. Keep your urinary system busy and your energy field clean by ingesting water. Working with appropriate crystals such as citrine, calcite, golden beryl, yellow tourmaline, and yellow calcite helps, as does visualizing crystal clear glowing yellow light in your solar plexus and in a bubble around your body. Say to yourself:

"I RECEIVE
the light of the Macroverse
by cleansing and purifying my solar plexus chakra
with yellow light energy.
I AM RECEPTIVE."

8th Chakra
HEART CHAKRA
PINK

"I LOVE"

Circulation ✦ Compassion ✦ Circulatory System ✦
Love Energy Out ✦ "Light Becomes Love"

The 8th chakra is the heart chakra and it vibrates to the energy "as above, so below." While the 7th chakra receives, the 8th chakra gives. The 8th chakra transforms light into love before sending it out with Compassion to all life. Sending love energy out into the world is extremely important, not only for the survival of the Macroverse, but also for your own survival and health. The heart chakra's energy is pink, and it is associated with the circulatory system of the body. Just as the heart pumps lifeblood through the body, so does the heart chakra pump love energy out into the body of the Macroverse.

We know that the modern-day 7-chakra system associates the heart chakra with the color green. This is primarily for two reasons: (1) there was a distinct need to infiltrate the Earth reality with an overflow of heart energy and people's association with green encouraged the growth of heart energy, which accomplished this purpose; and (2) because the 7-chakra system did not account for the thymus or breath chakra (associated with the color green), the heart and thymus were often confused. Our guess is that intuitively, you have easily associated the heart with the color pink for a reason. The heart vibrates to the color pink, a soft, loving color that represents a mixture of blood and spirit, or energy of the 5th and 13th chakras, representing entry (birth) and exit (death/transformation) points for the human body. Pink is also the color of compassion and is associated with positive, kind, loving, and generous energy.

The love energy of the 8th chakra is necessary not only for optimum health but survival as well. Circulating love energy is important to manifesting a happy, healthy, and compassionate world. The heart chakra is your true power center. It is the point where all energies—upper and lower, outward and inward—merge. It symbolizes the reflection of self and the connection to All That Is. To energize and balance this chakra, it is best to utilize glowing, radiant pink light and associated pink stones such as rose quartz, kunzite, pink agate, and pink tourmaline. Say to yourself:

**"I LOVE
all life with compassion
by energizing and balancing my heart chakra
with glowing pink light energy.
I AM LOVING."**

9th Chakra
BREATH CHAKRA
GREEN

"I BREATHE"

Thymus ✦ Balance ✦ Immune System ✦ Nature ✦
"Breath of Life"

The 9th chakra is a new chakra for many people, and it is called the thymus or breath chakra. The significance of breath has been understood in a number of cultures as well as in modern-day yoga culture. Breath is automatic; it does not require conscious thought. However, with conscious awareness, breath can be harnessed for a variety of activities. This is called the Breath Chakra because it is located in the middle of the breastbone, between the lungs. Although breath moves down into the abdomen and out through the mouth or nostrils, the thymus is the point in the body signifying breath. Imagine this chakra as a butterfly, with its body as the thymus or breath chakra and the wings as the lungs.

 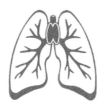 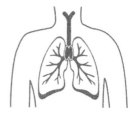

This is your 9th chakra. Breath is the fundamental motion of the entire Universe of Space and Time. Everything in the universe breathes, including the universe itself. Understanding breath is essential to understanding the fundamental movement of all life in the universe. It is the movement of air into and out of your body. Consider air for a moment. What *is* air? Well, you know it is necessary for your survival and for the optimum functioning of your body. You breathe in oxygen and you breathe out carbon dioxide. Plants, on the other hand, breathe in carbon dioxide and release oxygen. It is a perfect symbiotic relationship, like the interlocking spirals of your DNA.

Breath is about balance. The right amount in, the right amount out. Your body *knows* how to take oxygen from the air and how to release carbon dioxide. You do not have to think about it. It does it naturally. The thymus is responsible for creating a natural balance of positive cells and negative cells inside the body. The immune system is closely associated with the 9th chakra and keeps a healthy balance in the body by identifying and weeding out the disharmonious cells and reproducing healthy cells. What you may not know is that breath is essential to proper immune system functioning. Thus, should a person have an immune disorder, the first order of medicine by the doctor should be breathing exercises. Varied and adaptive breathing techniques can be utilized to boost immune system performance.

The color of the 9th chakra is bright, glowing green—a color of vitality and health. It is closely associated with growth and the natural process of evolution. It also represents Earth and plant life, reminding you that the oxygen plants produce is the oxygen humans need. To energize the breath chakra, it is important to go outside and spend quiet time in nature. Listen to nature, breathe with nature, and balance yourself. The chakra is located in the center of the breastbone and is also activated with green light and coordinating stones such as emerald, jade, dioptase, and malachite. As you visualize joining in with the breath of Earth, say to yourself:

"I BREATHE
the air of life
as I energize my breath chakra
with the vibrant green energy of nature.
I AM BREATHING."

10th Chakra
SOUND CHAKRA
BLUE

"I SOUND"

Throat ✦ Vibration ✦ Vocal Expression ✦
"Signature Vibration"

The 10th chakra is the throat chakra and is associated with the creation of sound. In religious and historical texts, you will notice that sound is closely associated with the act of creation. From the Judeo-Christian Bible, you may remember the phrase, *"And the Word was made Flesh."* In Hinduism, the most sacred symbol represents the sound of creation: A-U-M. Of course, it is not a coincidence that this is similar to the mythological name of the first human, "Adam."

Sound, or vibration, is part of all life. Everything and everybody has their own song, or more accurately, their "signature vibration." This vibration is also closely related to sacred geometry, for sound creates sacred geometric patterns. So just as you can hear your own sound or signature vibration, you can also see it in a geometric formation. Everything can be identified by this unique vibration, and much will be discovered once humans are able to identify and read signature vibrations. In fact, signature vibrations will unlock *many* things. For example, the signature vibration of healthy cells in a particular part of the body can be replicated once it is known. This will allow for early detection and easy correction of disease.

Not only is sound integral to creation, but it is also intricately connected to self-expression. The ability to express yourself vocally is quite empowering and one of the most beautiful attributes of existence. Think of the birds in the morning singing their beautiful song. This is their expression, their voice, their mantra. Similarly, consider the power of the words you use. You now know that it is important to choose your words wisely because the vibration and intention behind words will manifest into form. Know that this goes far beyond language; intention is intricately connected to sound. The sounds you make represent intention expressed through vibration and will travel through the waters of Earth and your body to amplify and manifest that intention. Speak with care, for sound is one of the most powerful tools in the Macroverse.

To energize the throat chakra, send brilliant blue light to the center of your throat while sounding your note. Spend time getting to know your note and what it feels like to sound it out into the Macroverse. It is also recommended that you place light-blue or blue-green stones such as angelite, chrysocolla, celestite, aquamarine, and turquoise on your 10th chakra while sounding your vibration. Say to yourself:

"I SOUND
my signature vibration

**while energizing my throat chakra
with brilliant blue crystal energy.
I AM SOUNDING MY NOTE."**

11th Chakra
HARMONY CHAKRA
INDIGO

"I HARMONIZE"

Hearing ✦ Hormonal Balance ✦ Endocrine System ✦
"Radiant Opus"

The 11th chakra is the harmony chakra and is new for those trained in the 7-chakra system. The harmony chakra is associated with the hypothalamic-pituitary-gonadal (HPG) axis. This is the part of the brain responsible for homeostasis, among other things. "Homeostasis" simply means keeping the body in harmony with itself. The 11th chakra is closely connected to the body's endocrine system and the regulation and use of hormones throughout the body. Hormones are like musical notes sent out by the body to keep a harmonious tune. When the body gets out of tune, this area of the brain sends out the right musical note (hormone) to keep everything working properly.

The location of the 11th chakra is best identified by the point where the spine and the brain meet. It is in line with the ears, or just under the nose, or right below the mastoid process in the back of the skull. You can imagine this energy center resting in the middle of the indention between the nose and the lips. From this central energy point, envision vortices or cones of energy moving outward through each ear. These cones create a torus or a bubble of light around the body.

From the 11th chakra, harmony is created in the body with appropriate hormone release. Interestingly, this is the physical area where musical harmony is *heard* by the human ears. The purpose of the harmony chakra is to create balance and harmonious relationships among all energy centers of the body. It is associated with the master number 11 and the letter H which represents two individual energies connected together by a bridge, creating unity through harmony. If you consider that all of existence is a musical symphony, a radiant opus, then you will understand the importance of hearing the music and contributing your own harmonic frequency.

The color associated with the harmony chakra is indigo, a perfect blend of brilliant blue and glowing violet. The 11th chakra is energized by listening to beautiful music or vibrational harmonics while placing coordinating stones such as lapis lazuli, sapphire, azurite, iolite, and tanzanite around the four points comprising this energy center, as shown in the image below.

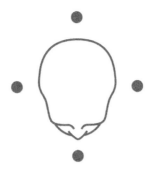

[TOP VIEW]

[FRONT VIEW]

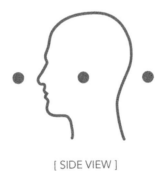

[SIDE VIEW]

Say to yourself:

"I HARMONIZE
with the symphony of existence
by listening to beautiful music
while energizing my harmony chakra
with indigo crystal stones.
I AM HARMONIOUS."

12th Chakra
ALL-SEEING EYE CHAKRA
VIOLET

"I SEE"

Third Eye ✦ Pineal Gland ✦ Psychic Center ✦ Intuition ✦
"Truth Beyond Illusion"

The 12th chakra is the third-eye chakra, or the all-seeing eye. It represents not only the psychic energy body but also the foundation of all intuitive sight. It is closely associated with the pineal gland of the body and has been referred to as the spiritual center or seat of the soul in modern chakra terminology. There are many associations between this chakra and the pinecone, from which the pineal gland was named to identify its shape. The pinecone contains intricate geometric patterns and is itself a geometric shape of some significance. You would be wise to contemplate the purpose and importance of a pinecone.

Ancient mythology has associated the pinecone with the Tree of Knowledge and suggests that it may be the fruit of the tree eaten by Eve in the Garden of Eden. What knowledge does a pinecone hold, and why would it be identified in the Judeo-Christian tradition as the very thing causing the downfall of humankind? In reference to the pineal gland alone, this would make sense because the third eye is the doorway to the nonphysical realms and provides a perspective on life different from the view through your physical eyes. If you consider the words "physics" and the word "psychic," you will see that the words have the same letters but in different arrangements:

P-S-Y-C-H-I-C

P-H-Y-S-I-C-S

If the all-seeing eye or the psychic body allows you to see everything as it really is instead of as an illusion, then perhaps the physical world moved some things around to create an illusion. If you can re-arrange the letters, you will see beyond the illusion into the truth of what is. Now, if you consider a closed lotus flower or a lotus just beginning to open, you will see a striking resemblance to the pinecone.

Photo © iStockphoto.com   Photo © iStockphoto.com

You will also notice the pinecone is used in ancient mythology as a key for creating or unlocking. It was used in Sumerian mythology:

Photo © Bigstockphoto.com

Photo © Bigstockphoto.com

And in Greek mythology:

Photo © HumanRecord.com

And in Christian art. In fact, the largest pinecone statue in the world is located inside the Vatican. Why?

Photo © Bigstockphoto.com

Photo © Bigstockphoto.com

Here is another representation of the pinecone that may prove to be quite interesting as you consider the 12th chakra.

Photo © HumanRecord.com

This is a vintage rendition of an ancient Sumerian artifact. A full view of this shows what could be interpreted as two creator gods using pinecones almost like keys or fertilizers to create something that bears a striking resemblance to the human energy body or the

Tree of Life. We do not wish to bog you down in ancient symbology; however, the importance of the pinecone cannot be understated. The fact that the pineal gland resembles and was named after a pinecone is no coincidence. Consider the following comparison between the widely-recognized Egyptian "Eye of Horus" and a cross-section of the human pineal gland:

Photo Credit: Encephalous Incursion, www.encephalous.tumblr.com

The pineal gland and the all-seeing eye are one in the same. The key to sight, to vision, to understanding, and ultimately to Truth, lies in the ability to see all. To see from a vista from where no secrets are kept. This is the key to Truth.

The pineal gland and the third-eye chakra are energized by the color violet and focused meditation. Violet light targeted in the third eye can awaken the 12th chakra, as can appropriately placed coordinating crystals such as amethyst, charoite, and sugalite. While in this state of focused meditation, say to yourself:

"I SEE
beyond my physical reality
by energizing my third-eye chakra
through violet energy and focused meditation.
I AM ALL-SEEING."

13th Chakra
CROWN CHAKRA
WHITE

"I AM"

Radiant Aura ✦ Lotus Flower ✦ Perpetual Growth ✦
Imagination ✦ "Rainbow Crystal"

Clark Hawgood, *Diamond Chakra* (2012), www.clarkhawgood.com

The final chakra for our examination is known as the crown chakra. This has strong associations with the diamond and the thousand-petal lotus flower. The 13th chakra is located at the center of the top of the head. It is where the human energy body opens up like a thousand-petaled lotus to connect with the higher realms and the higher self. It represents the full expression of evolutionary development in a human being. This is why saints and gods of mythology were often depicted wearing crowns or having glowing auras above their heads.

This was representative of a fully developed crown chakra and the optimum expression of human evolutionary development.

The crown chakra is most often associated with white light, although it would more accurately be associated with multifaceted diamond-like crystal clear light with a radiant aura. The full expression of the rainbow bridge comes to life through the 13th chakra, representing the crowning achievement of spiritual development in human form. The crown chakra is connected to the mystical and sacred number 13 representing the edges of the known Macroverse. Ultimate expansion of the 13th dimension of the Macroverse comes from the exercise and utilization of imagination. This is also true for the 13th energy center of the human body. To energize, develop, and grow the crown chakra, you must focus on accessing the edges of Truth and creating something beyond those edges. This is evolutionary expansion. This is the imagination. This is the meaning of eternity, perpetual growth, and discovery.

To expand the development of the 13th chakra, place a diamond or beautiful quartz crystal on the crown of the head or just above the crown if lying on the floor. Alternatively, white opal or anything exhibiting qualities of rainbow crystal, such as natural light shining through a multifaceted crystal or prism, can be used. It can be helpful to imagine white light focused on the crown of the head as well as all around the body. Focusing on the number 13 while intending to utilize the imagination is also useful in activating this chakra. While doing this, say to yourself:

**"I AM
eternal and constantly growing
as I exercise my imagination
and focus rainbow-crystal light on my crown chakra.
I AM ETERNAL."**

6

SACRED GEOMETRY:

THE KEY TO UNLOCKING THE CODE

A small part can hold the wonder of all things,
if you learn to locate the code,
the key, and the frequency from which to experience it.[14]

M ost life in the Macroverse does not speak a conventional language like humans do. Indeed, most thoughts are conveyed energetically, without the need for words. However, if we were pressed to identify a common dialect among existence, we would say that the language of harmonics is the interconnected and unifying expression of being. Harmonics may be defined as the musical pattern or energetic signature identifying every unique aspect of existence. For example, your universe is not called "the Universe of Space and Time" by the rest of life in the Macroverse. Such language is unique to human beings. Instead, the rest of the Macroverse identifies your universe energetically by harmonic patterns of light, color, and sound. These

---

14 Barbara Marciniak, *Family of Light* (Rochester, VT: Bear & Company Publishing, 1999), 202.

harmonic patterns can be easily translated into binary codes or mathematical systems. Thus, you could say that harmonics is also geometric, for it is an expression of identity in a spatial relationship to the rest of existence. All life in the Macroverse exists in *relationship* to all other life. It is this relativity that enables us to define life. Although we are interconnected in the unity of existence, each life form carries with it a distinct perspective. These perspectives provide us with the colors and flavors of existence. We refer to these unique points of view as *harmonic frequency.*

Harmonic frequency, or what we call "general harmonics," is a broad identifier of life utilizing unique vibratory expressions. Sacred geometry, however, is a subset of general harmonics because its meaning transcends a simple energetic signature or beautiful harmonic pattern. In fact, what sets sacred geometry apart from general harmonics is its *coding.* Sacred geometric patterns are forms encoded with vast amounts of information. While you might define general harmonics as *identifying signatures* such as beautiful mandalas or energetic "names," you could think of sacred geometry as *computer chips* filled with extensive amounts of high-frequency information. In fact, the information contained within a single sacred geometric pattern could fill up entire libraries on Earth. It could take lifetimes to communicate a message contained within a single sacred geometric pattern using the conscious mind. In fact, you could say that every sacred geometric formation is a computer chip connected with the "great computer" known as the Akashic Library. The Akashic Library includes all information from all perspectives from the beginning to the end and, of course, beyond the notion of both beginning and end. While each pattern encompasses a unique focus, all patterns act as gateways into this great library of All That Is. As you have probably noticed, these encyclopedic libraries, or geometric computer chips can be found all over your planet and throughout your universe:

Photo © iStockphoto.com

Photo © iStockphoto.com

95

Photo © iStockphoto.com

Photo © iStockphoto.com

In fact, some of your galactic neighbors have even used sacred geometry to download messages directly into the cells of your body via crop circles:

Copyright Steve Alexander Photography, www.temporarytemples.co.uk

Copyright Steve Alexander Photography, www.temporarytemples.co.uk

Copyright Steve Alexander Photography, www.temporarytemples.co.uk

Why does the Macroverse prefer this method of communication? It is, in fact, a simple and efficient way of communicating intricate concepts and multidimensional messages without the need for conventional language. Sacred geometry speaks directly to the essence of your being, avoiding interference from the ego and the conscious mind. So, understanding sacred geometry is like learning a new language—the interdimensional language of light.

The Process of Absorption

This brings us to our next point: exactly how are sacred geometric patterns used to communicate? The answer is simple: through *absorption*. The process of absorption is not widely understood by humans at this moment; however, it is widely used by humans on an unconscious level. Think about how much better you feel after spending quality time in nature. Why is this? It is because your body is *absorbing* healing energy directly from the plants, trees, flowers, mountains or ocean. Consider how much better you feel after spending only a few minutes outside in the sun. This is because your cells have just received a "download" of information from the sun. Information is integrated into your body from the sun through the process of absorption. Think about how you feel after eating a meal. Your body absorbs detailed information from the food you ingest. This is why it is so important to energize or bless your food before eating. This is also why you feel better when you eat raw, organic, and fresh foods. Cleaner foods allow the information contained within them to be easily conveyed and quickly absorbed by your body.

Some humans joke about "learning through osmosis" by falling asleep on your textbooks. In truth, osmosis is very real and simply another name for absorption. However, absorbing information from a textbook is a long and arduous process, for it contains information constructed solely for the conscious mind. Information contained within nature—the sun, the moon, the ocean, trees, and flowers— is *designed* for communication via absorption. The same is true of sacred geometry, for you receive and integrate this information directly through the cells of your body. It is designed to bypass your conscious mind. This is also true of the Water Code. The information contained within each water molecule inside your body is a code designed for release through the process of absorption, literally revealing its message to you from the inside out.

Infinite Reflection

As you may remember from your science classes in school, a water molecule is composed of two hydrogen atoms and one oxygen atom, giving it the chemical name of H_2O.

OXYGEN

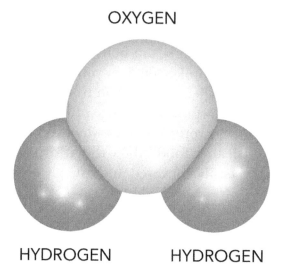

HYDROGEN   HYDROGEN

The hydrogen atoms are bonded to the oxygen atom, forming a triangle or pyramid-type shape.

In fact, you could think of the water molecule as bubbles inside a pyramid or as a pyramid inside of bubbles. As an atom bonds with another atom, we remember that everything exists in *relation* to something else. The statement "as above, so below" gently reminds us that beyond every pyramid we see exists a diamond.

And beyond every bubble exists an infinity symbol.

Photo © Bigstockphoto.com | NASA's Goddard Space Flight Center, *Fermi Bubble*

This is the manifestation of being as well as its reflection. In fact, you could say it is the representation of both being and non-being, the yin and the yang, the *is* and the *is not*. As the reflection of all life previously veiled from your perception fills the expanse of your vision, you will understand that in knowing the whole, you become part of the fabric. For the pattern of creation begins with relation to another as well as the reflection of the self. This reflection is infinite, extending inward and outward and into all dimensions of being and non-being. Thus, there is no end to this pattern, and an examination of each shape is potentially eternal, for there exist patterns within patterns within patterns within patterns...

It is also important to know that balance exists within all life. Although it seems that the flowing structure of the infinity symbol closely resembles water, the harmonic pattern for water is, in fact, the interlocking diamond. You have heard the phrase, "things are not what they seem to be," and this is quite true, for what exists beyond the veil is often the opposite of what you might expect. You could say that the diamond symbol represents an energetic balancing of what you know to be true and the full expression of Truth. Thus, for the purposes of our exploration into sacred geometry, consider that what you know of the "flowing" nature of water and the "piercing" nature of light may represent only half of the Truth. In fact, we would ask you to consider that the opposite is also true. To balance your perception with that which you have not yet perceived, consider the sacred geometric symbol for light, the infinity symbol, and the sacred geometric symbol for water, an interlocking diamond:

LIGHT

WATER

Light represents the expression of life, the experience of being, a manner of sharing energy with existence. It is a state of expanding outward from a singular point. Thus the infinity symbol for light is also the basic representative shape of universes and dimensions, and also of the Macroverse itself. As you may remember from the book *Divine Macroverse*, the basic structure of the Macroverse consists of 13 interlocking infinity symbols:

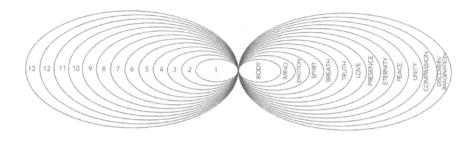

These 13 dimensions represent the 13 realms, or states of being:

1. Body
2. Mind
3. Emotion
4. Spirit
5. Breath
6. Truth
7. Love
8. Presence
9. Eternity
10. Peace
11. Unity
12. Compassion
13. Imagination

Integrating this structure, or sacred geometric pattern, into your conscious mind has enormous implications for your evolutionary development and the expansion of your awareness. This geometric structure provides you with a vantage point from which to reach new heights in your evolutionary awakening.

The Water Code

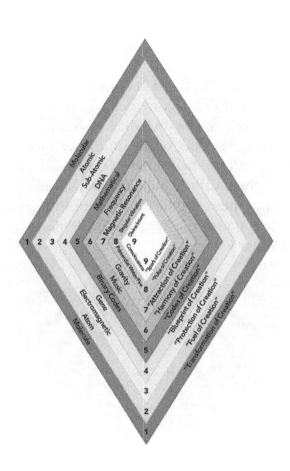

The sacred geometric pattern known as the Water Code exists at the quantum level, so it cannot be seen by the human eye. This code contains information concerning the true history of the planet, humanity, and all life on Earth since the formation of your universe. In fact, you could say the Water Code contains Earth's Akashic Records, dating back billions of years. Considering that your written records are only a few thousand years old, you can imagine the enormous amount of information opening up to you now.

An understanding of the sacred geometric structure of the Water Code is necessary in order to move to the next step—unlocking the code. The Water Code consists of 9 diamonds within diamonds, representing the 9 inner realms, or the fundamental structure known as "the Microverse." The Microverse is comprised of the 9 realms of non-being, sometimes called the "underworld" in ancient cultures. We will delve into these realms in depth in the next chapter. For now, we provide you with the names of the 9 quantum realms that comprise the Water Code:

1. Molecular
2. Atomic
3. Subatomic
4. DNA
5. Mathematical
6. Frequency
7. Magnetic resonance
8. Singular vibration
9. Divine intent

We invite you to absorb the information contained within the Water Code by meditating on its sacred geometric symbol:

Imagine the Water Code situated in the center of every water molecule within your body:

The Key

Now that you have taken a moment to integrate the Water Code into the molecules of your being, it is time to reveal to you the "Key" for accessing this Akashic computer chip. It should not surprise you to learn that the Key to unlocking one sacred geometric pattern is contained within another harmonic pattern. Thus, the Key to unlocking the Water Code involves integrating *a new harmonic pattern* into every cell of your body through the process of absorption. It is with great pleasure that we reveal this new harmonic pattern to you—the Key to unlocking the Water Code inside of you:

The sacred geometric pattern symbolizes the *integration of light and water*. It is the harmonious interrelationship of the sacred geometry of the Macroverse and the sacred geometry of the Microverse. This geometric structure unlocks the Water Code and releases information stored deep within your being and deep within Earth. This pattern bridges the frequency between water and light, creating a new geometric structure representing the connection between the inner and the outer. This symbol represents the revelation of the unseen that was previously veiled from human perception. You could say that this sacred geometric symbol bridges the *Freedom of expression* with the *Truth of introspection*.

LIGHT (FREEDOM) + WATER (TRUTH) =
NEW HARMONIC PATTERN

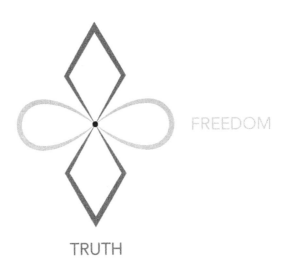

The Apex

Clark Hawgood, *Apex Gateway* (2011), www.clarkhawgood.com

The Macro- and Microverse connect to each other at a point of origin known as "the Apex." The Apex represents the space from which all creation was made manifest. It also serves as a portal to the multidimensional realms. Understanding and learning to navigate the Apex may well be the most important scientific focus of your lifetime. In fact, you could consider the Apex to be *the* gateway between the ex-pression of being into the im-pression of non-being. This is the point where the 13 infinity-shaped dimensions of the Macroverse meet the 9 diamond-shaped inner realms of the Microverse. Out of the Apex emerge both 13 and 9.

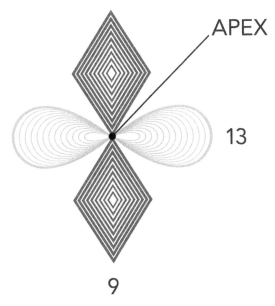

APEX

13

9

Understanding and focusing on the Apex when integrating this new harmonic pattern into your being is quite important, for it is out of this point that Truth emerges. Consider that in the center of every black hole is an Apex point, or a gateway from the Macroversal dimensions to the quantum realms. A black hole is a veil between the outer and inner worlds. Consider a water droplet moving through this veil. On the "outer" side, or Macroverse, the droplet expands into infinite light, spreading into space to experience a multidimensional, sensory expression of life. As the droplet moves through the black hole to the other side, it moves into the inner realms by traveling into itself, thus, seeming to disappear. However, the droplet has simply moved into the Microverse, or the quantum realms that exist well beyond the third-dimensional notions of space and time.

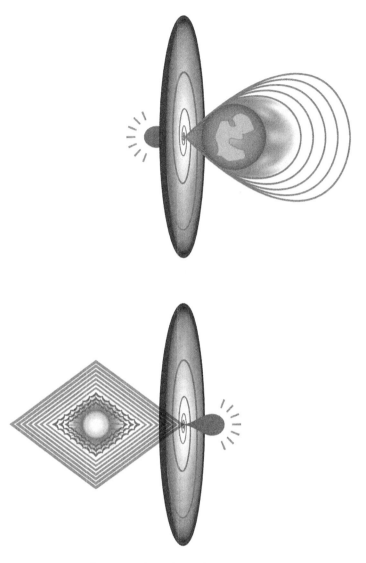

Humans are presently experiencing the outer planes, or the dimensions of being. Thus, it seems as if moving through a black hole takes you nowhere or is a gateway to nothingness, like being lost. This is just a limited perspective. What is a star imploding? What does that mean? It may appear to destroy itself. It may appear to lose its power, or its expression of being. This may be accurate from certain perspectives. In truth, "implosion" is simply evidence left behind in the Macroverse, of the exploration into the Microverse.

What appears as destruction from the human perspective is actually physical proof of the exploration into the quantum realms. This represents the movement from being to non-being, the journey inward to the point of creation, the birth of essence, and the return home. It is the expression of impression, and it is the impression of expression.

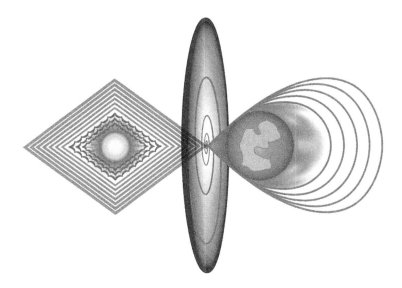

Geometric Fabric of Creation

To understand the significance of the code you are unlocking, consider what it means to uncover the Truth. You may have heard that a single human being's awakening affects all human beings because all life is interconnected through energy. This is, of course, accurate, although there is a more detailed explanation for this phenomenon that we would like for you to understand. This information we are sharing with you now will facilitate your ability to communicate instantaneously with any and all life on the planet. This will happen not simply as a result of a vague notion of interconnectedness but instead with conscious use of the geometric grids surrounding your planet and your physical body.

Presently, two primary grids exist in your reality—the Light Grid and the Water Grid. Both grids allow for instantaneous communication through an interconnected vibrational pattern surrounding Earth. These geometric grids represent the harmonic interconnection of the two fundamental substances of creation: light and water. Thus, together, these grids form the Geometric Fabric of Creation. For some time, these grids have been working independently, holding separate and distinct focuses. This has not been advantageous for life on Earth, and we are most grateful that this truth is changing. Before we talk about the geometric integration, let us explore the Light and Water Grids in greater depth.

The Water Grid

We invite you to consider the interconnected geometry of water from a two-dimensional perspective:

And next from a three-dimensional perspective:

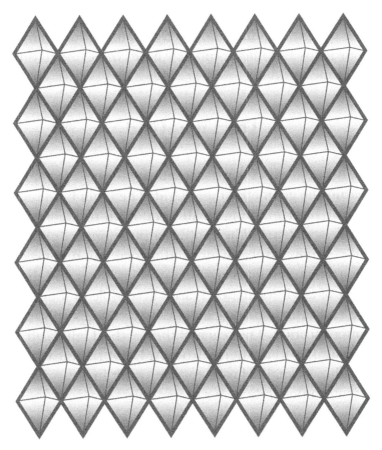

In actuality, the geometric fabric of water is multidimensional, extending in every direction, in, around, and through all things. Though you cannot see this fabric with your physical eyes, these interlocking, multidimensional diamonds surround not only Earth but also your personal energy field. Each diamond represents the relationship of the inverted pyramid, often perceived as the chalice or the feminine symbol, to the pyramid, or the masculine symbol. As such, the diamond acts as a unified doorway to the inner realms, effectively encompassing both feminine and masculine to create a gateway into the wholeness of being, or oneness. At the present moment, the Water Grid acts independently as a communicator between extraplanetary, extrauniversal, and extradimensional life and the Earth energies that are presently tapped into this grid. Dolphins, whales, and other oceanic life regularly use the Water

Grid to communicate with their families in other realms. Depending on the quality and harmony of the water inside your body as well as your focus and intent, you may have connected to this Water Grid from time to time.

The Light Grid

Humanity usually operates in accordance with the information contained within the geometric Light Grid. The Light Grid represents the energetic intermingling of all light, both inside and outside of the visible spectrum. The sun has a huge impact on the Light Grid, and you have probably noticed a correlation between solar events, such as coronal mass ejections or solar flares, and the quality and content of the information readily accessible to your conscious mind. Presently, the planetary Light Grid facilitates only intraplanetary communication. The reach of the Earth's Light Grid is easily adjustable, similar to changing from AM/FM radio to satellite or Internet radio. A small adjustment can result in a vast increase in communication possibilities for humanity.

To begin, it is helpful to think of the geometric fabric of the Light Grid as interlocking infinity symbols:

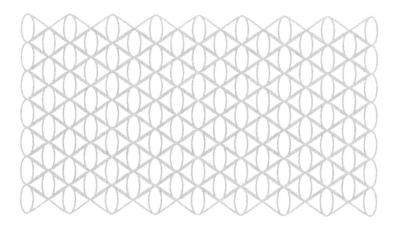

From a greater dimensional perspective, however, you would see that the infinity symbols are actually interlocking cones of light energy:

Light moves outward in a perpetually flowing infinity symbol, connecting infinity to infinity, or cone to cone. The Apex of the infinity symbol joins mirror images— as above, so below. Upon examination of the Light Grid, you see that the idea of a circle is merely a limited dimensional perspective of one side of a cone. As you broaden your perspective of the Light Grid, you will notice the ends of infinity symbols overlapping in a bridge-like pattern similar to a double helix of DNA. These bridges form important pathways for light to move into and out of various states of conscious awareness.

Integrated Light and Water Grid

The key to exponentially expanded communication rests with the overlay of the two planetary grids. This act of uniting the grids in your imagination and then, in your reality, is an important step to accessing greater Truth and Freedom for all planetary life. Most important, an Integrated Light and Water Grid creates a structure for instantaneous communication among all life on Earth, free from outside interference and the need for technology. An integrated grid is essential to the principle of Truth. Accessibility to the Truth is an inseparable aspect of this fundamental right for all life in existence.

The harmonic pattern of light can be found at every Apex. From a two-dimensional perspective, the pattern of light looks like an infinity symbol. However, from a multidimensional perspective, it is more like a cone:

The geometric pattern of water can also be found at every Apex in the shape of connecting diamonds:

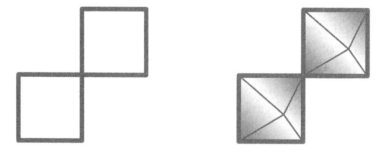

Thus, the harmonic patterns for both water and light come together at every Apex, forming a multidimensional structure that looks like this:

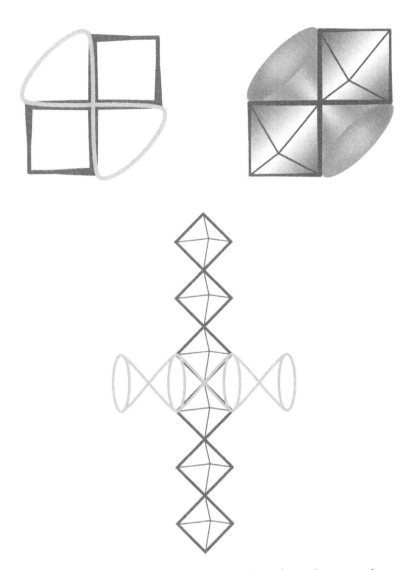

Remember, every Apex is a point of creation. Apex intersections represent the entry and exit points for information moving into and out of your collective reality. Thus, every Apex represents a crossing of the Light Grid and the Water Grid. For quite some time, these intersection points have been cordoned off, and the Light and Water Grids have operated separately. We are grateful that this is no longer true. Imagine the two grids connecting at every Apex. Visualize energy moving freely between the grids through these Apex points to bring these grids into union. Now, imagine the two patterns overlaid:

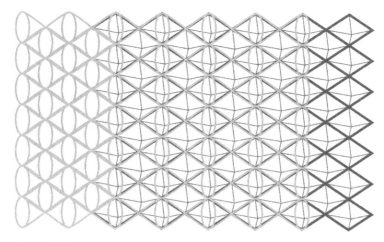

Or perhaps like this:

From every Apex in the Light Grid, you see the Water Grid, and from every Apex in the Water Grid, you see the interlocking infinity pattern of the Light Grid. Imagine this close up:

Now, imagine this intricate overlay from a multidimensional perspective:

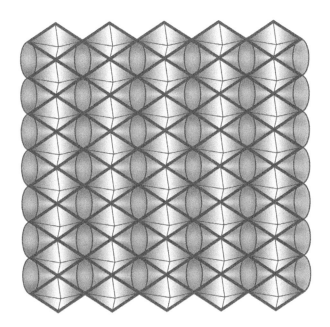

Or close up:

Now, if you look closely at the multidimensional Integrated Light and Water Grid, you will see the Key for unlocking the Water Code embedded in every Apex:

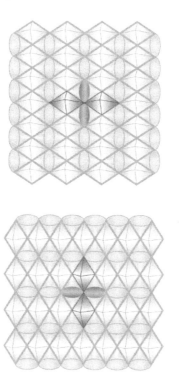

It is very important that you visualize the Key at every Apex intersection of the Interconnected Light and Water Grid. This Key will not only unlock numerous interdimensional, interuniversal and interplanetary portals facilitating clear and direct communication with your celestial neighbors, but it will also act to infuse the energy of light and water into the grids, ultimately integrating them into one harmonious planetary energy grid. This unlocking is the pathway to ultimate Truth and of course, Freedom for all life on Planet Earth.

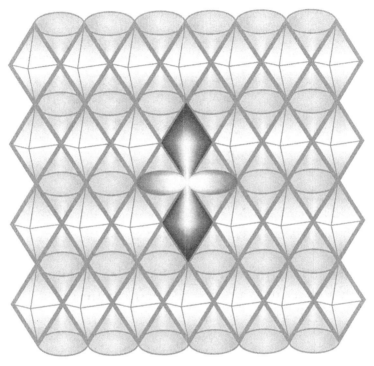

As you begin working with the Key, you will notice that this pattern has been embedded in the sacred geometry of all creation. As your awareness expands, you will begin to see this Key in all patterns, in everything around you.

Crop circle image: Copyright Steve Alexander Photography, www.temporarytemples.co.uk

Everywhere you look, you will see the Light Grid and the Water Grid integrating into a single, unified geometric pattern.

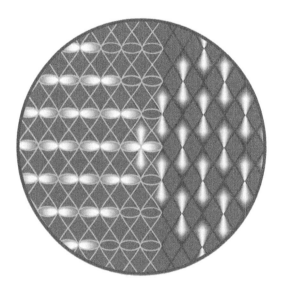

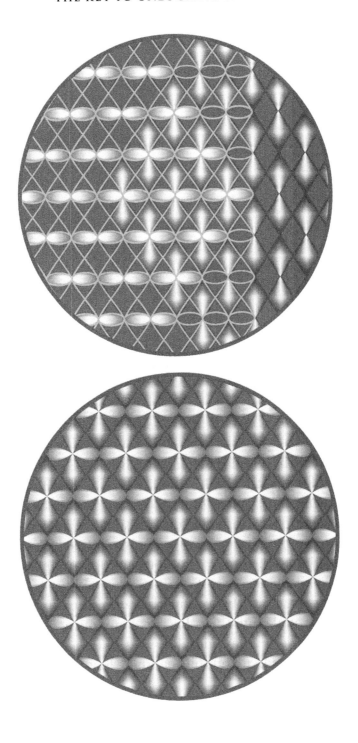

Key to Truth

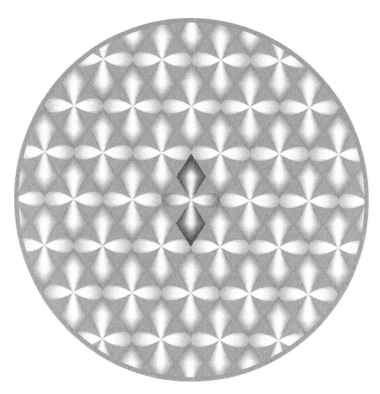

The "Key to Truth" mandala contains within it the sacred geometric codes for unlocking the truth within every water molecule in your body. Focusing on this mandala daily and meditating on it, will produce exceptional results in your personal life. Even using this mandala as your computer's wallpaper is an effective way to bring this information to the forefront of your mind. Your personal efforts to connect with the essence of this sacred geometric mandala will positively impact all life throughout the fabric of existence. Integration of this mandala into the collective consciousness is imperative in humanity's evolutionary development. We invite you to take a few moments to meditate on this mandala, focusing on it with your third eye.

Unlocking the Code Meditation

Now that you understand the harmonic pattern of creation forming the interconnected fabric from which the Key emerges, you have an understanding of the blueprint for all life. You also have the tool for unlocking and understanding this blueprint. Everything in your universe was created from light or water or some combination of the two. Thus, unlocking the Water Code also means unlocking the codes of creation. The code will reveal itself through the process of absorption. To begin the unlocking process, we invite you to implement the following steps:

1. **RELAXATION:** Enter into a state of deep relaxation by sitting or lying in a comfortable position. Close your eyes. Breathe in and imagine light entering your body from above your head, moving down your spine, and traveling into all of the cells of your body. As you exhale, imagine you are releasing from your body all of the energy and thoughts you do not want. Breathe in peace. Breathe out stress and worry. Breathe in color. Release any energy that is stuck or creating blockage in your body. Continue this process until you have reached a deep trance or meditative state.

2. **FOCUS:** With your eyes closed, focus on the Key in your mind's eye. See the gentle, expressive movement of golden light through the infinity shape and the internally impressive reflection of water through the concentric diamonds. See the 13 dimensional realms of the Macroverse represented by the concentric infinity symbols. Now see the double-diamond pattern of the Microverse and the 9 inner realms contained in it. Imagine overlaying the patterns so they come together at the Apex. Now move your focus to the Apex of the Key. Imagine going deeper and deeper inside the Apex. Hold this image in your mind's

eye for several minutes until you feel its imprint in your mind and in the cells of your body.

3. **CONNECTION**: Imagine a copper grounding cord coming out of the Apex of the Key and moving from your mind's eye into the cells of your body. Now imagine the molecules that make up each cell in your body. Watch the grounding cord move through your cells, searching for water molecules. The cord easily finds them, given that you are made primarily of water. Watch as the grounding cord invites the water molecules to create a connection. The water is excited to do this because it knows that the moment of revealing has arrived!

4. **OPENING:** See the water molecules open up in reflection, like the wings of a butterfly, preparing for the copper grounding cord of the new harmonic pattern to enter into the Apex of each water molecule. At the very center of the water molecule, you will see the sacred geometric pattern known as the Water Code.

5. **UNLOCKING:** Now imagine the copper grounding cord of the Key gently reaching inside the Apex of reflecting water molecules. The geometric patterns connect

Apex to Apex. As soon as the connection is made, every-thing lights up. In an instant, the new sacred geometric pattern is imprinted into the water molecule and inte-grated into the essence of water. The Key starts spinning inside each molecule. As it spins, the water transforms by integrating the new pattern into the very core of its essence. As it transforms, an unlocking occurs. A light emerges from the Apex and radiates outward through the boundary of each molecule and through every cell in your body until light pours out of your body, as if you are a glowing, radiant being of light.

PART TWO SUMMARY

In summary, to unlock the Water Code and receive water's revelation about the Truth of our existence, follow these simple steps:

1. Establish resonance with the frequency of water by raising your individual vibration. This can be achieved by:

   • Drinking harmonized water.
   • Adding Himalayan salt to the water you drink and the food you eat.
   • Applying Himalayan salt topically through salt misting and salt baths.
   • Receiving information from the sun while immersed in water (ocean, pool, bath, or shower).
   • Regularly moving salt water through your body using exercise, saunas, or steam rooms.
   • Using color as a mechanism for healing, clearing, and awakening.

2. Balance and energize your 13-Chakra Energy System using the 13 Chakra Intentions.

3. Remember that sacred geometry is the Key to unlocking the Water Code.

   • Water is identified by a sacred harmonic pattern.
   • This pattern contains within it encoded information called "the Water Code."
   • The Water Code contains the full and complete history of the Earth and all life on the planet, also known as Earth's Akashic Records.
   • This code is unlocked with a specific geometric pattern called "the Key."
   • To unlock the Water Code with the Key, perform the Unlocking Meditation, as detailed in chapter 6.

4. Repeat Steps 1 through 3 until you feel that the Water Code has been successfully unlocked and you are ready to explore the revelations of water.

5. Receive revelations from water as you gain access to this storehouse of information previously veiled from humanity's conscious perception. The process of receiving personal revelations from water is explored in part three, "The Water Code Revealed."

PART THREE:
THE WATER CODE REVEALED

7

THE 9 QUANTUM REALMS
OF THE MICROVERSE

The emergence of the diamond from the coal
teaches the creation miracle of
transformation, transmutation and transfiguration.[15]

Clark Hawgood, *Water Diamond* (2011), www.clarkhawgood.com

15   Sharon Shane, *Architects of Light* (N.p: Liquid Light Center, 2004), 149.

Congratulations! You have successfully unlocked the Water Code. Unlocking the Water Code is equivalent to opening the door to the greatest library you have ever known— Earth's Akashic Library. The library is vast, expansive, and awe-inspiring. It could take eons, eternity even, to completely uncover everything contained in this library. Water will assist in this exploration by sharing its sacred "books," the Water Code collection, with you. This information has been guarded, protected, and encoded until this special moment when humanity and water reach a resonant vibration. Now it is time for the Water Code to be revealed.

Within these books lies the essence of water's message—that the quantum realms are the next frontier in human exploration. You may wonder how something so "small" could be so important. Remember, what you see with your physical eyes is only a tiny fraction of what is. Existence is everywhere, all around you, in front of you, behind you, inside of you, and in many realms awaiting your exploration. The quantum realms are where Earth's Akashic Records can be found. Contemporary human history relies on records dating back only a few thousand years, but consider the fact that Earth has been around for billions of years. Think of what you do not know just about Earth alone! Imagine the feeling of directly experiencing Earth's ancient events instead of simply reading about them. Learning to navigate these realms means having the ability to acquire Truth on your own, without the need for an intermediary such as written records. This is the gift of the Water Code. Water is teaching you how to access the Truth, stored deep inside you, in the quantum realms.

Simplifying the Quantum Journey

We know that many people's eyes glaze over when they read about quantum mechanics and quantum physics. These are presently the domain of modern science, which is not accessible to many human beings because of its primitive expression. What you will soon discover is that the most evolved concepts in science are actually the simplest. Truth should be easily had and universally translatable. There are some present-day Earth scientists, specifically in the field of quantum physics, who are successfully translating scientific concepts to the masses, and this is a wonderful evolutionary development.

With these thoughts in mind, consider that "quantum" simply refers to ingredients, or a careful combination of energies designed to create life. These ingredients reside in the dimensions of non-being. What does this mean? How can something *not* be? Consider what it means to "be." You *are*. Well, you *are* what? You *are* experiencing life, and you *are* aware that you are having this experience. In fact, you are guiding and exploring and enjoying the experience of life. Now, if you are not doing this—if you are not "being"—then what? You are experiencing life but without consciously participating in it. You are participating in life but not *observing* the experience. Instead, you are *becoming* the experience. You are *not* being. You *are*. A state of "non-being" does not mean that you are dead or not moving or somehow not participating in life. If "being" represents the outward expression of living, then "non-being" is the inner expression of living. Life on the inside is quite simply life on the other side.

To better understand this, consider the experience of breath. All life breathes without conscious effort. It is a basic function of life. The yogis from the East invite meditators to follow their breath. This is very good advice and is, in fact, the beginning of the journey into non-being. You cannot see the air you breathe, yet you know it is there. How do you know this? Well, there is evidence supporting the concept of breath. As your lungs expand, you can feel the breath moving into your body. Your exhale moves air out into the world around you, where you observe its movement affecting matter in its path. Your inhale moves air back into your body, giving you energy, strength, and liveliness. Thus, it is with this awareness of breath that you are able to understand the realms you cannot see and cannot experience with the traditional five human senses. How do you comprehend something you cannot see, hear, smell, taste, or touch? You experience the quantum realms because you *are* the quantum realms. You are part of them and they are part of you.

Similarly, you could say the functions of the body provide evidence for the quantum realms. Imagine that you are by yourself on a deserted island. You have lost all memory of your former life. You have amnesia. What is the very first thing you will remember? Probably that you are thirsty and would like to drink water. Do you think you would remember to eat or to sleep next? Well, you would not have to think much about it because your biological needs would be driven by physical urges in your body. You do not need to think too much about this information because it lives inside you. The Microverse is not an external concept for your brain to understand, for it is much deeper than that. In fact, the best way to understand the quantum realms is to absorb the information into your energetic body, allowing it to reveal itself to you from the inside.

Journey Through the Microverse Visualization

When describing something entirely new, we think it is helpful to activate the imagination through visualization. Let us take you on a journey through the 9 Realms of the Microverse:

1. **Molecular**
2. **Atomic**
3. **Subatomic**
4. **DNA**
5. **Mathematical**
6. **Frequency**
7. **Magnetic resonance**
8. **Singular vibration**
9. **Divine intent**

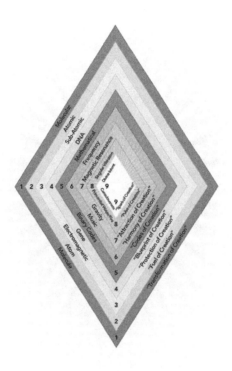

In this journey, we will follow the rainbow colors of realms 1 through 9, moving inward toward the spark of creation—the beginning of life and the first expression of existence. The rainbow represents the path of traveling inward. Just as you follow the rainbow to the mythical pot of gold, so too does the rainbow take you from the dimensions of being into the depths of creation.

What lies at the end of the rainbow bridge is a fantastic treasure, for it is the birthplace of Consciousness. It represents the very origin of life itself. We invite you to take a moment and focus on the diamond rainbow fabric representing the quantum realms. Look at it, absorb it, and allow it to blend with your cellular consciousness. Do not try to make sense of it. Just focus on the image without thinking for three minutes.

We are ready to begin. Now, close your eyes and take a moment to focus on your breath. Your belly rises slowly and steadily with the in breath and falls into relaxation on the out breath. As you continue your slow, steady breathing, remember that your physical body is evidence of the quantum realms, revealing their intricate dance of musical resonance and intentional design. Let us imagine ourselves as part of the breath, part of the air moving into our lungs and dispersing as oxygen throughout every cell of the body. Let us follow this oxygen, this purposeful energy, into a single cell. Perhaps it is one of the cells of the human heart. What does this cell look like? Is it round, like a bubble? What color is it? Do you see it pulsing in unison with the other cells of the heart, creating the steady percussion of the heartbeat?

Consider the purpose of the heart. The heart sets the time for the human body. As you know, time is a mechanism for understanding the spatial relationship of things to other things. It is a tool for measurement. It provides structure. The heart also acts as the central organ for the circulatory system. It is responsible for moving lifeblood through the body. It pumps it and keeps it moving. This is its *design*. Every heart cell has this focus and makes a perfect effort to live up to this purpose or mission.

Let us imagine going *inside* the heart cell. What comprises the heart cell? Do you see the millions of molecules making up just one heart cell? How are they moving? Do you see an increase in movement or energy? Are the molecules moving together, or does their movement appear more chaotic? Imagine that these molecules are the *fuel* for the heart cell. They are creating energy through movement, so they move very quickly. That is their purpose—to create as much energy as possible to fuel the heart cell.

Now select a molecule and journey inside it. Does the rapid pace of the molecular world seem to disappear? It feels very far off now, does it not? Like moving off a busy highway into a serene country pasture. You look around and see it is simple. Do you see one atom or two? How are they moving? Perhaps they are barely moving. You may notice a slight vibration, similar to a humming sound. Very subtle. You like it here. Everything is clear. What is the purpose of the atom? You could think of it like a house. It is a place of safety, security, and order. The purpose of the atom is to provide strength and order, a house for the energy created by the molecule. What is in this house? Go inside.

The first thing you notice inside of this atom is sound. There is a very distinct sound of electrons and protons moving around the nucleus. You have reached the subatomic level, a realm of electro-magnetic direction. The nucleus holds the blueprints for the heart cell deep within it. It is necessary for the nucleus to have protection; thus the electrons were created to shield the nucleus. The subatomic realm is really the protective shield. The sound produced by the subatomic particles shields the nucleus.

Now let us journey through the nucleus of the atom, into the DNA of the heart cell. This is what you call a "gene." A gene is a detailed blueprint of a particular creation. It is the architecture of the creation. The DNA you have encountered looks kind of like a spiral staircase and is really not understood by modern science. Think of a blueprint. What is its purpose? To account for every detail and every ingredient so that all the materials are integrated perfectly to form the desired outcome. Part of the reason human scientists do not understand DNA is because most of it is dormant. Think of a blueprint for a house and consider that you are only looking at the first page of the plans. There are 12 more pages of information right behind the first page that you are not seeing. Looking at DNA like a spiral staircase is part of the problem. DNA is multidimensional and quite intricate. It spins and moves, connecting purposefully in 13 specific points that provide access to each layer of the plan. This is the point where modern science has reached an impasse. Let us move beyond this limited perception.

Start with the spiral staircase. Do you see the 13 intersections, what might appear to be a criss-cross? These are entry points. Let us select an entry point and move into it. How about the sixth entry point? Go inside of this point. What do you see? Numeric codes are all around you. It is quiet here. You see white space all around and binary codes everywhere, almost floating in white space, beside, behind, above, and below. It looks like numeric soup. What is the purpose of these binary codes, you may wonder? To carry and release information as needed to form the intelligence behind the blueprint. When you think about it logically, everything you experience is either "1" or "not 1" or some combination of these. Being and non-being. Mathematical codes measure and express this scientific truth.

Now look at the 1s and 0s. Select a 1 and go inside of it. What do you see? What do you hear? There is a pattern, almost like music or a song. Do you see a geometric pattern? It is like looking through a kaleidoscope—you see the colorful patterns of musical sound. There is a beauty and a flow to the 6th realm. This makes perfect sense since this is where music originates. Now listen carefully to the song. Select a particular sound within the music and go inside of that. Perhaps it is a chime. What is behind the sound of a chime?

If you go inside the sound of a chime, you may notice a sort of "pulling together" to form the sound. What creates the sound of the chime? Is it the attraction of like sounds? Is this attraction the force behind the chime that creates the sound? You have just entered the 7th realm of magnetic resonance. It is here that gravity in its purest form exists. For what is gravity really but attraction? Why are things attracted to each other? Because they relate. And why do things relate to each other? Because they have resonance. Like attracts like at this level of the quantum realms. This magnetic resonance is fundamental to the creation of beautiful music. Without attraction, music would not have harmony and would instead be chaotic noise.

Let us go inside the resonant parts. What do you see or feel or hear? Can you find the singular vibration? Go inside of the singular vibration. What do you find? What created this vibration? You may look around and see a vast ocean. Many have called this the primordial waters of creation. Do you see fire or the first expression of light? Where is it? Is it in the water or separate from the water? Can you tell? It is very quiet and calm here in the 8th realm. You are inside the womb of All That Is. Water is swirling and fire is swirling, like gentle soup. They seem to be separate but reflecting each other. Parallel, you might say.

Go into the center of the swirling water or swirling fire. What is there? Vastness. Endless eternity. Nothing. Everything. Beyond stillness. Beyond physicality. Beyond openness. What do you see at the very center? At the very center is a tiny, tiny particle of light. It is the spark of creation. Divine intention. It is the first flicker of Consciousness, of awareness, of the desire to relate. If you go into the spark, you will find nothing, for oneness cannot observe itself. Congratulate yourself, for you have just journeyed through the 9 Realms of the Microverse. Now we will explore these realms in greater detail, beginning with the birth of Consciousness and moving outward.

Quintessence:
Pre-Conscious Light

Clark Hawgood, *Quintessence* (2011), www.clarkhawgood.com

In our "Journey through the Microverse," we traveled into the center of the Microverse—the very heart of the rainbow diamond. You may wonder what exists beyond the realm of divine intent. The answer is infinity, for more always exists beyond the beyond. With that in mind, however, we would like to explore the source out of which Consciousness was born.

It would be accurate to say that Consciousness is light, for light is the beginning of All That Is. But what preceded light? Where did light come from? Light, in fact, came from liquid light, with no conscious awareness of itself or existence. Thus, you could say that liquid light without awareness birthed Conscious light. We call this liquid light Quintessence, or *Pre*-Consciousness. You might wonder if Quintessence is the same as oneness. Because there exists no *awareness* of oneness, Quintessence is *pre*-oneness. The idea of oneness is created from the notion of nonseparation or nonindividuality, which requires comparison, or Consciousness. Quintessence precedes awareness. It is beyond the quantum dimensions. It precedes both the Microverse and the Macroverse. In fact, Quintessence precedes all notions. It is beyond description because to describe it gives it Consciousness. For now, let us say it is "beyond the beyond."

We invite you to be present with the idea of Quintessence, for if you follow the path inward, into the heart and essence of every cell or particle in your body, it will lead you to this place. Can you imagine light without Consciousness? Can you imagine the Source of creation? Perhaps this is further than you have ever imagined? We invite you to gain comfort with this exercise, for the journey inward is ultimately the path to truly knowing yourself. We were all born of Source, and the journey inward will always lead us back home—into the beyond the beyond.

Realm 9: Divine Intent
Birth of Consciousness

It was out of Quintessence that Consciousness was born. This is the heart of the diamond and the first flicker of life emerging from Quintessence. We call this the "spark of creation." This is the 9th and most fundamental realm of the Microverse, often referred to as "divine intent." Born from beyond the beyond, the first imaginative spark represents the "Birth of Consciousness" and the creative process. In fact, you could say realm 9 symbolizes the:

BIRTH OF LIGHT

From beyond the beyond, came a flicker, a spark, a point of light. From Quintessence, Consciousness was born. Consciousness is also referred to as awareness. Pre-Conscious light became aware of its existence because of the *desire to create*. For awareness is truly the first step in the creative process and the beginning of the journey from intention to manifestation. The 9th realm of the Microverse is where light gained conscious awareness of itself and began the adventure of self-exploration. The very act of developing conscious awareness is born from the desire, or intent, to create. This leads us to the first expression of creation found in realm 8 of the Microverse.

Realm 8: Singular Vibration
Pulse of Creation

Photo © Bigstockphoto.com

As Consciousness awakened, it desired to express itself. The journey from the 9th to the 8th realm is the movement from *intention* to *expression*. The expression of Consciousness is exhibited as a singular vibration. You could refer to this first movement, or initial expression, as the "Pulse of Creation."

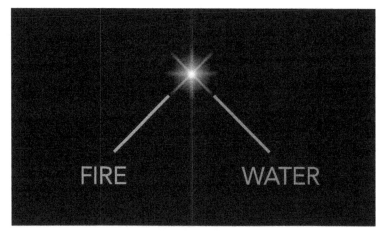

From divine intent, Consciousness was initially expressed as water, followed closely by fire. We call these initial expressions of Consciousness, Primordial Water and Primordial Fire. This expression was not a competition or a race. In fact, their expression was not linear. They came about more like flower petals blooming. The petals began to open to reveal an intricate and beautiful center (water) and then continued opening and reaching outward into their full expression (fire).

Photo © iStockphoto.com   Photo © iStockphoto.com

This initial vibration, or expression of Consciousness, precedes resonance and thus does not hold any magnetic or gravitational force. Therefore, Primordial Water is quite different from the substance you know of as water on Earth. Water on the Earth exists in bodies, formed with resonant groupings of water molecules. Primordial Water precedes molecular structure by many realms and is representative of water energy in a state of complete oneness. Likewise, Primordial Fire is quite different from the substance you refer to as "fire" on Planet Earth. You might think of it as liquid lava but without any gravity—like floating, liquid fire. These primordial substances are a simple and very ancient expression of Consciousness itself.

The initial expression of Consciousness created a primordial tone we call the singular vibration. This is the pulse of creation, the first sign of life in the creative process and the identifying signature of the two most fundamental substances in existence—water and fire. The first sound of creation was "OM," representing the audible expression of water ("O") and fire ("M"). This singular vibration represents the full circle of creative expression, for the mouth opens to sound O and closes to complete the M. This symbolizes consummation, fullness, and balance. Like the inhale and exhale of breath, the primordial substances of water and fire represent the wholeness of creativity. OM is the signature vibration of all creation, reminding us that Primordial Water and Primordial Fire are the fundamental building blocks of all life; of everything and no-thing. The primordial expression of creation represented by the singular vibration of water and fire is best visualized by thinking of Primordial Water swirling clockwise and Primordial Fire spinning counter-clockwise, out of a single point of light (divine spark) and mirroring each other. We call this the vortex of creation:

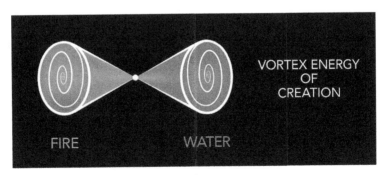

This vortex consists of the O and the M moving out of pure Consciousness, or divine intent. This creative vortex balances the primordial expression of Consciousness and allows these two energies to reflect on one another. From this vortex, the 7th realm came into being.

Realm 7: Magnetic Resonance
Attraction of Creation

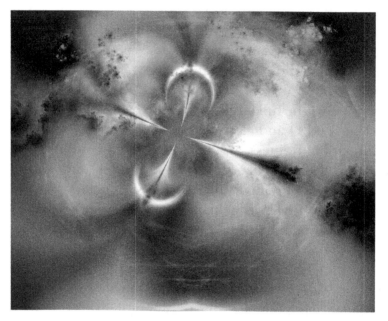

Photo © Bigstockphoto.com

Once the expression of Consciousness is made, the call for reunion begins in the 7th realm of the Microverse, known as magnetic resonance. We refer to this as the "Attraction of Creation." This fundamental attraction exists among all life, for magnetic resonance is ultimately the pull of all life back into one of the two primordial expressions of Consciousness—water or fire. We could see how this may be interpreted as the beginning of duality, or being pulled to one "team" or the other. However, water and fire are not in opposition, they are complementary. They represent two unique paths back to Quintessence.

Consider that magnetic resonance is the beginning of gravity, although in a much more fundamental form. Understanding that gravity represents the inherent attraction of all life back to fire or water will rapidly unlock many mysteries of modern science. While it may seem that all objects possess a gravitational pull towards other objects, you must remember that this only includes objects with mass (formed out of fire). Objects without mass were formed out of water, so they have no gravitational pull toward objects of mass.

It is also important to distinguish between magnetic resonance (gravity) and the return to Source. All life, including water and fire, possesses the inherent desire to return to the Source of divine intent. This is the energy of creation itself. In truth, the pull back to Source is stronger than the pull back to the creator. Although this terminology has religious overtones, you could say that light is Source, and water (or fire) is creator. It is the nature of life and all creation to know its origins, for in knowing where you come from, you are able to know who you are, what you are, and where you are headed.

Realm 6: Frequency
Harmony of Creation

Photo © Shutterstock.com

Magnetic resonance is the foundation underlying all harmonics. What is harmonious or disharmonious can ultimately be explained by an underlying gravitational pull toward water of fire, or Primordial Water or Fire. Realm 6 is the realm of frequency and the birthplace of harmony. It is where the vibratory expression of divine intent coupled with the fundamental attraction of creation developed into patterns of creative expression, or harmonic resonance. We call this realm the "Harmony of Creation." This realm of the Microverse is where blending begins. You might say this is where quantum "recipes" began, for the music of creation is simply the blending of frequency.

It is here in realm 6 of the Microverse, that harmonic patterns known as frequency were introduced, and it is here that music originated. Many refer to this realm as the music of Consciousness. In fact, music is one of the easiest ways to enter the quantum realms. You know when you hear a song and you can feel it "in your bones" or "deep in your soul"? This is the physical result of a quantum experience. Music is a direct pathway to the Microverse for it moves easily through the quantum dimensions, directly accessing the fundamental expression of Consciousness from which you were born. Music aligns with magnetic resonance, pulling you toward it, which is why you may feel music quite deeply in your being. Music comes from the blending of fire and water, forming resonant sound, resonant harmony and harmonic resonance.

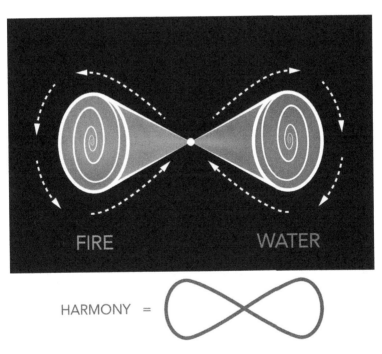

Realm 5: Mathematical Codes of Creation

As the music of the 6th realm moves into the 5th realm, you will notice that the music becomes orderly and arranges itself in binary codes. We refer to these mathematical patterns as the "Codes of Creation." This is the 5th realm of the Microverse: the mathematical realm. Many intricate and detailed manifestations came into form in this quantum realm. It takes a very high level of mastery to understand the creation codes. In Earth's history, these codes were only shared with initiates or sages of the highest vibration. Now, these codes are revealed to you.

We call the 5th realm of the Microverse, "mathematical" because all harmonic patterns are formed from fundamental mathematics. Perhaps more accurately, mathematics is a symbolic language describing the basic patterns of harmony. These patterns are formed from binary codes. All harmonic patterns can be described mathematically with a 1 and 0. This can also be expressed as "1" and "not 1," or "being" and "non-being."

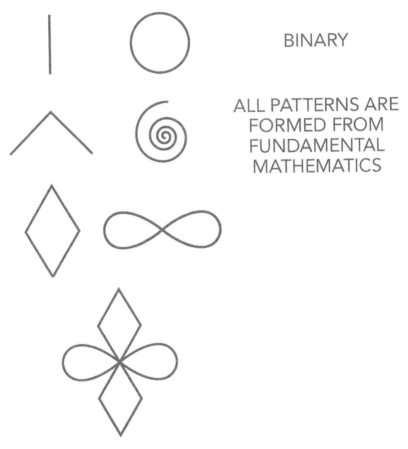

BINARY

ALL PATTERNS ARE
FORMED FROM
FUNDAMENTAL
MATHEMATICS

These binary codes express this scientific truth and are the intelligence behind the blueprint of creation.

Realm 4 - DNA
"Blueprint of Creation"

Photo © Shutterstock.com

Realm 4 is the location of DNA, the "Blueprint of Creation." This is where the binary coding of realm 5 combines into harmonic patterns useful for creating and building. You might say that DNA is the sacred language of manifestation and the architecture of life.

As we mentioned earlier, DNA accounts for every detail and every ingredient of creation so that all materials are integrated harmoniously to form the desired outcome. What humans are seeing as the spiral-staircase form known as DNA is actually only approximately 7 or 8 percent of the blueprint. In essence, scientists are only reading a tiny bit of what is really DNA. To fully understand the coding inside of you, it is necessary to change your perspective. Let us begin with an example. Consider the human eye:

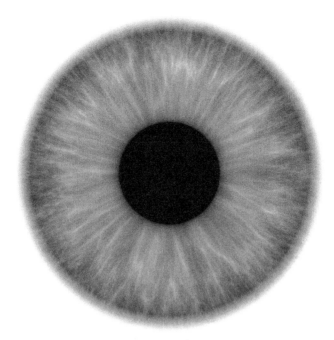

Photo © Bigstockphoto.com

From the outside, it looks like a circle or perhaps a sphere or bubble. However, when we look from a different perspective, we can see that the eye is shaped more like a cone.

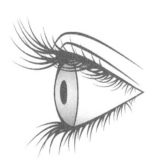 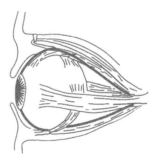

Understanding your DNA is quite similar. You see a simple "strand" of DNA, but this is a limited perspective. When you remember that everything is interconnected, you will consider the fabric holding DNA strands together.

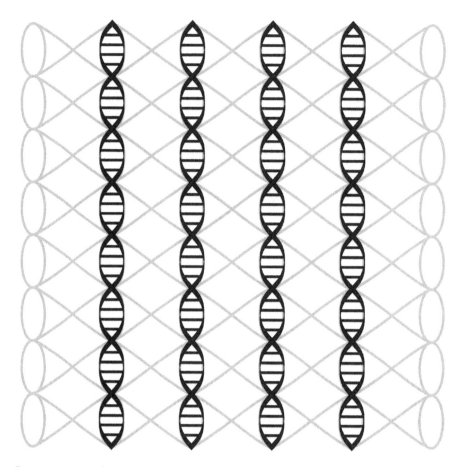

Once you understand that a DNA strand is simply part of a larger fabric, you will begin to consider the relationship of one DNA strand to another. How do they connect?

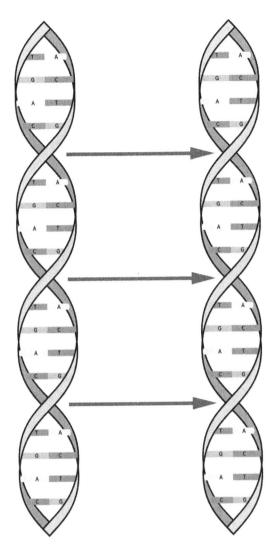

If you change perspectives as you did with the human eye, you will see that DNA strands are actually shaped more like interconnected cones.

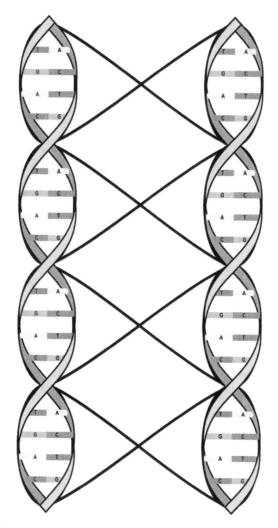

The image of a DNA strand is only one part of a cone. A more complete map of DNA might look like this:

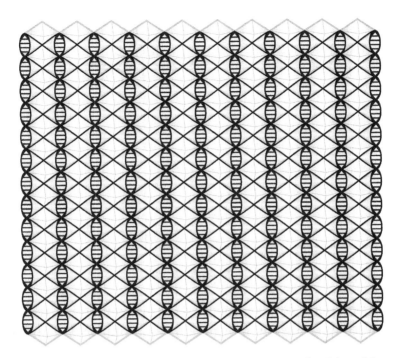

Instead of strands of DNA, you will see an interlocking blueprint that reveals the interrelationship of the cone structure, the missing information in previous interpretations of DNA. You will see the cone and diamond fabric of creation, and you will know that understanding this geometric pattern is essential to understanding all creation. In fact, a multidimensional DNA map is the key to resolving numerous health issues relating to the human body. Knowledge of the sacred geometric patterns you learned about in the last chapter will greatly assist you with this.

Do you remember the discussion of the significance of the Apex? In fact, healing and regeneration are both easily had with the appropriate use of the Apex. Consider the caduceus, an important symbol in alchemy and the staff carried by Hermes in Greek mythology:

Photo © iStockphoto.com

You will find many codes embedded in this symbol that are helpful in uncovering significant information from your DNA. Think about the 13 Chakras as discussed in part two of the book. Consider that each chakra represents an Apex. These same Apex points exist within your DNA. When you follow each cone shape back to the Apex, you will discover a doorway leading you to important answers for your physical health and longevity. This will involve returning the body to a healthy vibrational signature. To do this, the appropriate vibrational signature must return to zero point, and this requires a connection with the corresponding Apex.

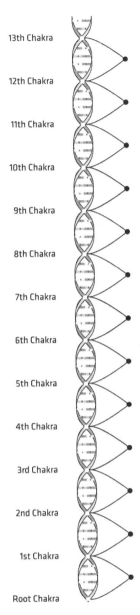

13th Chakra

12th Chakra

11th Chakra

10th Chakra

9th Chakra

8th Chakra

7th Chakra

6th Chakra

5th Chakra

4th Chakra

3rd Chakra

2nd Chakra

1st Chakra

Root Chakra

When you consider how the point of origin relates to the diamond pattern of water and the fabric of creation, you will unlock your DNA coding and uncover the purpose of what you had previously called "junk DNA."

Realm 3: Subatomic Protection of Creation

Photo © Bigstockphoto.com

The subatomic realm is where the coding was manifested into the first bubble of life. Each bubble of life is specifically designed with a protective energy field. Thus, creation is protected. We mentioned that DNA is kept in the nucleus of an atom. As we move into the 3rd realm of the Microverse, we move outward to explore the subatomic particles providing protection to the blueprint of creation. The subatomic realm is focused on sound and the utilization of sound to protect DNA coding as the blueprint manifests into form. You remember the biblical reference, *"And the Word was made Flesh,"* and in fact, this is quite accurate, for sound is an integral piece of the creation process. In addition to sound's creative function, certain sounds are effectively utilized to provide protection. In fact, sound is the key to creating and sustaining energetic shields.

Let us consider the particles within the subatomic realm. As you know, the nucleus of an atom is made up of protons and neutrons. Protons are positively charged particles and neutrons are neutral, not having any charge. Neutrons are sometimes referred to as the glue holding the positive particles in place. *Development* comes from the grouping of positive particles. *Protection* comes from the movement of negatively charged particles known as electrons.

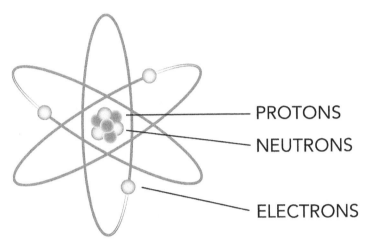

PROTONS

NEUTRONS

ELECTRONS

The nucleus is the birthplace of form. Note that form and non-being are not mutually exclusive. Because you are form does not mean you are *being*, and because you are non-form does not mean you are *non-being*. The main difference between being and non-being is that being is an outward expression and non-being is an inward exploration. Form and motion can exist in either state.

Consider the information that can be gained by simply looking inside the formation of an atom. Negative energy does not create new life. Instead, it *protects the creation* of new life. It provides an energetic shield so that new life can be created undisturbed by outside influences. It should be noted that electrons provide protection from *all* energy. Positive energy keeps out negative energy while negative energy keeps out all energy, both positive and negative. We invite you to take a moment to consider the implications of this truth.

Negative energy is not a necessary component of the creation of new life; it purely provides protection. New life is born from *positive energy*. When positive and negative energy are balanced, they can work *together* to form something beautiful. The frustration you feel in your human experience is that the positive and negative are not in balance. Thus, creation and protection are not working properly. This is simply corrected with an energetic rebalancing, which is what you are working on right now, in this very moment. Once the energetic rebalancing is complete, creative manifestation and harmonic protection will function properly. When this happens, the electromagnetic force of all creation will operate optimally.

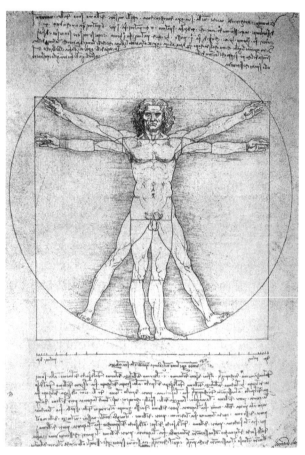

Photo © Bigstockphoto.com

Consider "electron shells," or the orbital pattern followed by electrons around the nucleus of an atom. You may notice that there are seven shells.

Now let us look at the electron shells and structures of different atoms. Here you will see hydrogen and helium, lithium and beryllium, boron, aluminum, silicon, titanium, and gallium, respectively.

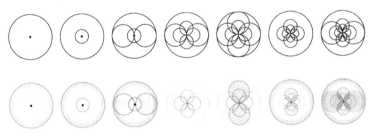

The electrons in these atoms utilize some or all of the shells to create specific patterns of frequency. You will see that the designs formed by the electrons represent the optimal electromagnetic pattern for the protection of the nucleus of that particular atom. You may also notice that these patterns correspond with sacred geometry. In fact, sacred geometry has much more to do with the quantum realms than the Macroversal dimensions of being.

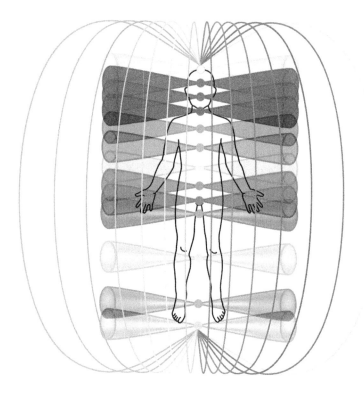

Now consider the electromagnetic field generated around the human body. As you know, this protective shield has not been working optimally. Of course, this field is created by your central energy centers, or chakras. Each of your 13 chakras creates a sort of electron shell around your body that can work as a very effective shield when patterned appropriately. The key to resolving the issues related to the proper protection and Freedom of human beings resides in the subatomic realm. Know that the 13 chakras are essential to fully understanding and, ultimately, resolving these problems.

Realm 2: Atomic
Fuel for Creation

Realm 2 of the Microverse is the atomic realm, also known as the "Fuel for Creation." The atomic realm is a place of great activity. It is the realm of energy generation. Quite literally, it is the fuel for life. The 2nd realm of the Microverse is where atoms move in relation to each other to create energy for the functioning of the greater molecular purpose, or the greater good, you might say.

Atoms are highly energetic, almost chaotic to the average observer. However, their movement is very deliberate and their intention is absolutely clear. You may wonder how such movement exists in the Microversal realms of non-being. We will remind you that non-being does not mean non-action. There is much activity in the quantum realms. Think of the ocean. Would you consider the ocean active? Of course! It is always moving, always transforming, always active. However, it is also sublime. Its purpose, or state of being, is highly energetic yet at the same time quite refined. Likewise, it may seem as if the atoms are bumping into each other, but this is not really the case. They are consciously utilizing the power of reverberation to create dynamic energy to fuel their molecular universes. Quite simply, atoms know that they can create more energy working together than alone. This understanding leads atoms to enjoy a highly interactive lifestyle.

Atoms are quite skilled in creating an ever-increasing surge of energy. Think of moving the volume up on your television. This is an *amplification* of sound. Amplification of energy can happen through the technique of grouping or through energetic reverberation. Presently, you think of reverberation as something related to the remnant of a sound event in an enclosed space.

In fact, it is not an echo or remnant of an event but the *extension* of an event caused by the continuous and conscious interaction of atoms moving in a particular space. So imagine a group of sound atoms (Group A) taking their energy and directing it into a group of wall atoms (Group B). This intentional and directed energy transfer amplifies the initial energy, causing the sound to extend longer than its normal life cycle. This is what you call a reverberation, or reverb. Thus, Group A can create an amplification of sound through the intentional and focused use of directed energy.

Now, a *conscious grouping* occurs when Group B decides to *respond* to Group A's amplification of energy through *conscious participation.* So, if the atoms in Group B were to join with Group A and move back toward the source of the sound, the initial sound would not only extend, but it would also grow louder. Thus, conscious grouping entails deliberate participation by all atoms involved. Both groups decide to join together and move toward a common goal. Once the combined group reaches the common destination, it recruits more atoms to the effort, and this energetic gathering creates the energy needed to propel the atoms back to the wall and then some. This extra energy is used to attract additional atoms and so the effect gets larger and larger, or more and more powerful. This is the process of *Energetic Reverberation.*

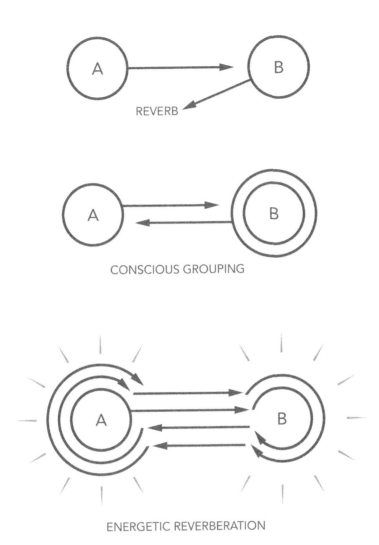

REVERB

CONSCIOUS GROUPING

ENERGETIC REVERBERATION

Atoms utilize the power of Energetic Reverberation to create an endless supply of energy to the molecular universe it calls home. On a practical level, this same process is helpful in understanding how humans could create "free energy" or what may be referred to as a bridge between realms. Inter-realm bridging is fundamental for optimal communication and unrivaled functionality. The atomic realm has many exciting secrets to share with you. We encourage you to fully explore the 2nd realm of the Microverse.

Realm 1: Molecular
Transformation of Creation

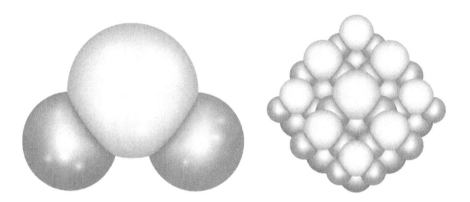

Realm 1 of the Microverse involves the "Transformation of Creation" from one state to another. This is the molecular realm and the bridge between the expression of being and non-being. Realm 1 is the quantum realm closest to the Macroversal dimensions of being. The first realm of the Microverse is often referred to as a place of germination, for it is here that life is fertilized for growth. This is the wonderful place where non-being is transformed into being. This is the beautiful pause before the breath, the space of possibility before the birth of form.

Molecules work together in a state of purposeful harmony, always focused and dedicated to their life mission. Molecules have a wonderful way of communicating with each other, and this is accomplished through a sort of osmosis. You could compare it to telepathy, although it is not the working of a mind. It is an absorption of information by other molecules within a certain proximity. It is an instantaneous and complete communication ideal for the greatest good of creation and, specifically, for the optimal expression of the molecular mission. Overall, the molecular realm is quite orderly and highly efficient. Similar to group consciousness, the molecular realm functions with purpose-driven teams. This realm is known for harmonious interrelationships and a mission-driven life experience. You could say that a molecule is a *pod* of atoms, similar to a pod of dolphins. Like dolphins, atoms group together to fulfill a molecular mission or group intention. They come together to fulfill sacred contracts.

Molecules enjoy a purpose-driven life. They achieve their life mission throughout the entirety of their life experience. They enjoy wonderful relationships with other members of their "tribe" or purpose group. They work together to improve efficiency and to overcome obstacles. It is a results-oriented life experience. Consider the crystals inside a natural geode. The outside shell is rock but the inside is composed of thousands of tiny shimmering crystals. These inner crystals provide a skeletal structure out of which the larger rock was formed. You would never know this without opening the rock to journey inside. You may look at a geode and think, "Oh, this is simply a rock." This is true of all matter. Many beautiful treasures from the quantum realms work together to create the structure of form. What you are actually witnessing is the evolution of existence through the expression of form and non-form. Think of molecules as the sparkling crystals possessing all of the gifts of the quantum realms held together by magnetic resonance and pulled into form by the force of the outward expression of divine intention. The magic of transformation awaits your exploration in the molecular realm of the Microverse.

Quantum Healing

We would like to take a moment to explore healing in the Microversal realms of the human body. A better understanding of the quantum realms is necessary for resolving issues for humans such as disease, illness, deterioration, and death. What you will discover is that most issues arise in the 6th realm (frequency), the music of the Microverse. This is where tiny fluctuations in harmony can be felt most intensely. Right now, you are beginning to have awareness of the emotional causes of disease or sickness. What you will discover is that emotions are intricately related to disruption of the body's harmonic frequency in the quantum realms. When the music is interrupted, it becomes very difficult to return to the harmonic pattern from prior to the disruption. This is because of the uniqueness of the music inside every human being. Like snowflakes, no two human frequencies are alike. Once a disruption occurs, that person must find a new pattern, and this is where many processes and functions break down.

You are discovering the importance of vibrational healing and how this is intricately connected to the water within your body. However, you may have noticed that simply placing a tuning fork on the disrupted area of the body does not provide absolute healing. Noticeable improvement can occur, yes, but there is a missing link. The reason for this is that you are adjusting the frequency of a *disrupted pattern*. Thus, you are not eliminating the disruptive pattern but instead integrating it into the new music. The key to resolving this disharmony is *resetting the frequency* before creating the new pattern.

You might think of this process as rebooting your computer. You must first shut down the disharmonious frequency. This can be accomplished by releasing the cellular memory of the harmonic pattern. To flush the quantum memory, you engage in something similar to time jumping. You must revert to a previous quantum expression, or what you might consider another timeline. Put simply, you move into the past to return to a healthy experience of the body. Humanity is on the verge of learning to time jump, so this will be much easier once that is accomplished. In the meantime, however, consider that everything has a vibratory signature. This means everything, down to the cells and into the quantum levels. If you could take a snapshot of your body when it was functioning optimally, let us say at early adulthood, and record the vibratory signature of your cells in key parts of your body, this snapshot would act as a sort of time machine. You could then use this time machine to reset the disharmonious cells to match their vibratory signature prior to the illness. In a way, acupuncture works at these levels, so that would be a good starting point for vibratory healing.

Coupled with the ability to reboot the frequency, physical adjustments to the body in the quantum levels are key to making real progress with healing. Perhaps someday you will create a sort of healing machine, something similar to an MRI but with acupuncture-type needles that connect with thousands of points on your body. These needles can function together, individually, or in groups as necessary to address a particular issue. Further, the needles can be adjusted to carry any frequency you would like into the quantum dimensions of a cell. They are also capable of carrying colored light into a cell as needed to focus on a particular problem. Additionally, the temperature of the needles can be adjusted, although temperature would be used primarily to deal with issues arising from the atomic levels. The bottom of the bed is made of water, almost like a waterbed, to simulate a womb. The person being treated by the machine does not get wet but is immersed in the bed of water without touching the bottom.

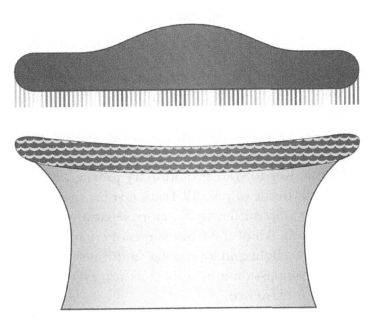

Perhaps you will build this quantum healing machine in the near future. In the meantime, there are ways to reboot your frequency but they are not 100 percent effective. You can immerse your body in water completely and then adjust the frequency of the water with sound, such as tuning forks. You could do this in a bathtub and use a breathing apparatus like a snorkel. A second or third person would need to work with the frequency of the water by holding the tuning forks on the sides of the tub, on the surface of the water, and slightly above the surface of the water. This procedure is effective because the immersion provides a complete structure for the frequency adjustment. Immersion also alerts the water cells inside the body to pay attention and assist with the frequency rebooting. The complete immersion provides a space free from Earth's gravity where different natural laws apply. The environment is more conducive to change and is controlled to some extent by the communication between the outer water and the inner water. In fact, communication with water is best achieved while submerged in water. This differs from simply putting a tuning fork on one part of your body, because when you do so, you receive only localized attention from a particular group of water molecules and not a holistic balancing. It is important for all of the water within the body to carry this new vibration into the quantum realms.

Many scientific and healing discoveries await you as you journey into the inner world— the 9 quantum realms of the Microverse. Remember to follow the diamond inward and always look for answers at the Apex point. The Apex reveals the bridge between light and water and the doorway from the Macroverse to the Microverse. It also holds the Key to your evolutionary journey. Know that all answers are really inside of you. All Truth is yours to experience. No more secrets. No more suffering. No more separation. A new reality reveals itself to you. All of the expressions of creation are yours to enjoy. We send you light and love, water and inner peace. We offer our gratitude, compassion and respect as you enjoy the Freedom and *Truth* of your existence.

8

EXPLORING EARTH'S AKASHIC LIBRARY: Q&A WITH REMI

All of you reading this are pioneers, for you would not be attracted to this information if you were not ahead of your time.[16]

What is the purpose of this book?

To unlock the quantum layers in your water essence. The gate is open; now you must learn to navigate these layers.

What is water's message for us?

Understand your origins, and you will understand your future. In some respects neither your future nor your past exist, and in some respects both exist right now simultaneously. Just as you are experiencing this moment right now, you are also experiencing your past and future and, of course, the infinite realms beyond time. Your experience of this present moment seems to be comprised of two variables:

---

16   Sanaya Roman, *Living with Joy* (Tiburon, CA: HJ Kramer, 1986), 24.

the impact of seemingly unrelated "outside" events (what you refer to as the "collective reality") as well as your individual perspective of the present moment. In fact, both are intricately interrelated and thus both impacted by your ability to transform your perception of reality. This is your task - to alter your perception to such a degree that *both* your personal interpretation of reality *and* the collective experience of reality are forever changed.

I hope this news is exciting for you, because I know how helpless you have felt, believing that you are somehow a powerless player in this collective experience, often waiting for the world to evolve, for the human frequency to increase, and for exponential change to manifest. What I am sharing with you, however, is that your personal evolutionary achievements can affect our collective reality much more quickly and significantly than ever before. This is because of the active participation of water. Water has joined you on this mission and, in fact, is dedicated to transforming Earth and this universe into a place of harmony. Water has agreed to assist you in spreading the good news. So please, Lightworkers everywhere, focus on you for a moment. Are you creating home all around you? Are you spreading love and compassion to every person you come in contact with? Are you experiencing joy? Are you growing, learning, and developing? Do you take the time to connect with the higher realms? Are you doing your part to bridge dimensions and frequencies? Are you transforming the patterns plaguing human-ity, one emotion at a time? I hope so. Water is spreading the good news instantaneously, creating an exponential impact for all life in the Macroverse.

What questions should we be asking?

How is water in your body related to the water in the ocean? What is the purpose of salt in ocean water? What is limiting human explo-ration of oceanic depths? What is water's relationship to the sun of the solar system? What does water have to reveal to us about the center of our universe? Could the center of the universe reside on quantum levels? If so, what exactly is this structure we perceive as the universe? What substances are able to travel from our realm through the quantum realms? How do we achieve unity with these substances? What is the true history of Earth, and why has it been kept hidden? How is information stored? How is it protected? How is it hidden? How can it be revealed? What does the advent of the Internet teach us about the nature of information? Why is it that although it seems like outer space should be filled with countless life forms, humanity is not consciously aware of any? Where is everybody? Is the physical body keeping us from space exploration or quantum navigation, or is something else holding us back? Why do our bodies seem so out of control? Why are we medicating our bodies to survive? Should we strive for liberation *from* our bodies or liberation *within* our bodies? What does the Egyptian ankh tell us about this question? What does the Christian cross tell us about humanity? What is the key to decoding our current human situation? What does it mean to re-veal se-crets? Sea-creations? What does the sea have to do with secrets? Why are humans kept separate from the oceans? How do humans gain harmony with the ocean? What does it mean to time travel? What does it mean to quantum travel? How does time exist in the quantum dimensions? Does it? What does time mean? What is multidimensionality? What is space? Do not ask the questions of someone else, *ask yourself.* Listen to the answers you receive from yourself. Learn to trust the wisdom of the water that lives within you, for it *is* you.

If we are made up primarily of water, why do we feel separate from water?

Although you *are* water, in a sense you have been separated from yourselves. Now is the time for revealing. You are removing the energetic veil that has kept you separate from the Truth inside of you. Consider the structure of a water molecule—it is very defined and actually quite minute. Water exists primarily in the quantum realms, yet you see only a portion, a tiny fraction, in 3D. What is important to note is that water is similar to your essence, or your spirit, because only a small portion of who you are is able to come into form at this density. In this environment, it is difficult to bring such energy into the physical experience. Consider that the water molecules that make up your entire body are 85 to 90 percent quantum, and think about your composition across dimensions. You are quite expansive, encompassing numerous dimensions and qualities not yet in your spectrum of consciousness. And so it is quite understandable that humans would feel separate given the veil between the physical and other dimensions. This is quite necessary, for the laws of *physics* or *physicality* impose certain restrictions, a structure of sorts, an environment for form and matter to exist and experience a perspective—a life experience. You may find it interesting that there are many ways to experience a perspective. These include techniques and experiences that expand far beyond what you would consider a "life." You think that you will pass on from this life into another life and then another, yet this is only one perspective. You can experience other worlds and other lives by visitation, not incarnation, arriving through the dimension of the imagination and also through absorption, a process that is beginning to make its way into your conscious perception.

Therefore, understanding water is fundamental to so many things. A deeper understanding of water is key not only to unlocking ancient Earth records but also to opening the lines of communication with interdimensional beings and all life forms across the Macroverse and the Microverse. Water is a communicator, a translator. Water is the genius inside of us, the creative force, the path inward, and the path beyond. It is the key to wisdom, to understanding, to knowing. And now this marvelous and extraordinary substance would like to come forward. You may feel it inside of you. Answers are coming to the surface. Little hints and clues are all around you, awaiting your awakening to the *divinity within you*. What do you think that means? It means you are comprised of ethereal, transdimensional, divine life force material.

What is the purpose of water?

Consider the physical appearance of water. How would you describe it? Translucent? Reflective? Would you say that water is blue? Often water appears blue to humans because its true color is outside of the visible color spectrum. Typically, water's appearance reveals no specific color, only a reflection of the color it encounters. What does this tell us about water's purpose? You could say the reflective nature of water is merely a "coating" that represents the "skin" of water. To discover the purpose of water, to truly know the essence of water, you must consider the aura, or color overtones, of water. Have you ever given a water reading?

No. I have never even heard of a water reading. What is it?

A water reading is similar to a human aura reading, except that you are reading the aura of water. Although water is interconnected, every water molecule is unique. You could say that groups of water molecules with a similar purpose will stick together. The color of water's aura will reveal the purpose of particular groupings of water. When you can read the aura of water, you will understand how to best use that water. For example, some water is best for healing, some for purification and some for gaining information. When possible, it is suggested that you harmonize your water before attempting a water reading. Environmental conditions and disharmonious frequencies can alter the outer energetic fields of water, affecting your ability to give an accurate reading.*

A water reading consists of several steps:

1. Connecting with the water molecules inside of a living being or inside of a glass of water.
2. Presenting the water with energy of love and gratitude.
3. Developing a resonant vibration with the water molecules.

---

* You can follow the steps for harmonizing your water that appear in chapter 4.

4. Listening to the water molecules. What do you hear? Words? A song? Music?
5. Asking the water to reveal its aura (color overtones) to you.
6. Understanding the message that the colors reveal.

When you see certain color overtones in water, you should consider the following aura colors of water:

PINK: This is nurturing water meant for energetic, emotional, and environmental healing.

MAGENTA: This is highly charged water and can be used for manifestation, creation, and new beginnings.

RED: Designed for purifying toxicity, this water is energetically potent. This potency allows it to combat and neutralize any toxic elements it encounters. Exercise caution with red-aura water.

ORANGE: This is magnetic water used to attract like energy. It is important to be very clear in thought, intent, and focus when in the presence of orange-aura water.

YELLOW: This water possesses cleansing qualities designed to remove impurities gently through the infusion of increased light. It is excellent for gentle healing.

GREEN: Growth-focused, this water is excellent for feeding growing plants. It can also assist with greater understanding, expansion, and development.

LIGHT BLUE: These molecules are the record keepers. Access to light-blue aura water is limited and a rare gift for the physical body. This water is great for accessing interdimensional planes.

BLUE: Blue is the color of the angelic realms. It is a guardian water meant to protect, guide and keep safe.

INDIGO: Indigo-aura water is known for expanding vision. It facilitates access to many realms and experiences and is also useful in sparking revelations.

PURPLE: This is birthing water, useful in multiplication and amplification. The purpose of this water is to replicate and expand.

WHITE: This is purification water designed for energetic cleansing and neutralizing. White-aura water creates a blank slate, assisting the user in gaining a new start.

BLACK: This water possesses information that is not yet accessible, typically because of energetic resonance requirements. Black-aura water is not useful to humans because it falls outside the human spectrum of vision.

RAINBOW: Water possessing a multitude of colors is the highest vibrational expression of water accessible to humans. This water adds harmony to all life around it.

How is it energetically possible to communicate with water when it is so different in frequency from our own?

You are correct that such communication is difficult, if not impossible, due to the Macroversal Law of Resonance. Put simply, this means that similar things relate to each other while dissimilar things do not. In fact, water is making a leap of faith, you could say, and attempting to transmute its energy to resonate more closely to your frequency. It does, however, request that you participate by raising your energetic frequency. Now, more than ever, it is imperative that you maintain the purest thoughts, the highest degree of joy, a heart full of compassion, and an expectation of miracles in every moment.

Are Earth's oceans polluted? Do we need to purify the energy of the ocean before attempting communication with water?

There is much waste and many unnatural chemicals in the ocean. However, water is not contaminated. It is intact. Only the energetic field surrounding water is affected by this pollution. So, yes, to communicate effectively with all of the water around the world, it is best to purify the energy of the oceans first, just as it is best to purify the waters of the human body. What you are really accomplishing is resonance with water through harmony.

Can water reveal its code in a polluted environment?

Yes. Water is much more powerful than the pollution surrounding it.

So it is not necessary to purify water first?

It is not necessary, but it is advised. This is primarily because the pollution surrounding a water molecule can disrupt a transmission of energy sent out by water. The pollution often distorts the information so the message is then misinterpreted by its recipient.

REMI, could you explain "water blending"?

Certainly. For you to gain a greater understanding of water blending consider "outer space." At this time, scientists believe that space is made up of mostly dark matter, although they are still speculating what dark matter is. Like 90 percent of your brain and 80 percent of your DNA, dark matter falls into a large category of "that which is not yet understood." You could say that water blends make up the majority of "that which is not yet understood." Let's start with dark matter. Dark matter is a blend of water and matter, or more simply, a recipe with a little fire and a lot of water. As humans raise their vibration, information relating to mysterious phenomena such as water blends will come to light. At higher frequencies, water is able to blend with other substances. These blends respond differently to certain "laws" of physics due to both the fundamental makeup of water and the operation of Macroversal and universal laws at higher frequencies. For example, water blends respond differently to gravity than other substances in the universe because water is not bound by gravitational laws. Many new scientific discoveries await you. Water blending is one of them. Vibrational physics—an understanding of how scientific principles operate differently at different frequencies—is another. Soon, humans will be able to evaluate and compare the vibrational frequencies of all things, including thoughts, emotions, and creative endeavors. The frequencies of Earth and different structures in space will be easily identified. The high vibratory frequency of dark matter will be discovered and will then be understood.

Although water blending is new to you, it is widely used throughout the Macroverse. In fact, many great things are produced with water as a key ingredient:

FIRE + WATER = MATTER

AIR + WATER = SPIRIT

LIGHT + WATER = ENERGETIC PATHWAY

SOUND + WATER = FUNDAMENTAL VIBRATION

WATER + FIRE + HARMONY = LOVE

WATER + FIRE + LOVE + SOUND = MUSIC

WATER + LIGHT + SOUND = KEY TO PORTAL NAVIGATION

Right now you see the spectrum of colors created when light hits water and you know it is beautiful. You might call it a rainbow bridge. What is it a bridge to? This is the beginning of interdimensional bridging and the foundation for multidimensional travel.

The blending of energies can be tricky, so it is advisable to establish a resonant frequency for this blending to occur. In essence, this prepares your water for blending. The initial step is to neutralize its vibration. Next, create a fundamental vibration. This act evens everything out so that a point of creation is made. Similar to "OM," as the fundamental vibration in musical notes, a point of creation is an essential starting point for all water blends. To establish a point of creation for the blending process, you should:

- Use water that is free from energetic imprinting. Take pure spring water and place it in a crystal or glass container along with a cleansed clear quartz crystal. To purify the quartz before use, rinse it in warm water, and then burn sage all around it (above it, under it, and to its sides) until all energy has been removed from the energetic imprint of the crystal. Rinse the crystal again and dry it before adding it to the pure spring water. Let the water sit overnight, ideally in direct moonlight. (Note that sunlight *adds* energy to water while moonlight *removes* disharmonious energies from water.)

- Pour the neutralized water in a large clear glass bowl. At the bottom of the bowl in the center, place a large sphere of quartz crystal. The sphere must be at least four inches in diameter to work effectively. Make sure the water completely covers the quartz sphere before proceeding.

- Next, select the Fibonacci tuning fork 13/21. Create its vibration and touch it to the large quartz underwater. If you have the appropriate microscope, you can observe the water molecules moving and then neutralizing after using the tuning fork.

- Now that you have created a neutral beginning, it is time to add light. Sunlight is best. Situate the water so that sunlight is directed right into the quartz crystal for at least four hours.

Now that you have established a point of creation for the blending process, it is important to remember that water is a great magnifier. Water has the capability of magnifying other dimensions so that they can be seen from any reality. While you perceive three dimensions with your physical eyes, water can detect all 13 dimensions. To access and utilize water's magnifying qualities, it is a good idea to raise your personal vibration so that you are able to attain resonance with the higher frequencies of water.

Water blends sound like an interesting new area to explore. Thank you, REMI. I was wondering, could you discuss the significance of the quantum realms?

It is wise to know where you came from - where you originated. It is important to know what you are made of, what makes you *you*. Until now, you have only seen half the picture. In fact, until very recently, you had only seen one-third of half of the picture. Your vision is expanding exponentially. You have experienced a crash course in evolution of sorts. Much has been shared with you and it can be very difficult to accept all of this change. The fundamental structure of your world has shifted dramatically and you are being asked to look at your world in an entirely new way. It is a lot, but do not be afraid. So many exciting discoveries await you!

No offense, but molecules and atoms just never seemed that important.

Yes, and 25 years ago meditation did not seem that important, at least to most people on the planet. Can you imagine life without meditation now? Think of all the energetic concepts that have opened up to you through the exploration of meditation. Just about one decade ago, everyone was riding the wave of collective consciousness without any awareness of how unconscious action was guiding everything. Learning to create your own reality, or to affect change on the collective through intentional thoughts, emotions, and actions has really made a huge impact on society.

You are right, meditation did open us up to the energetic realms. Is this the same as the quantum realms?

No. The energetic realms are the unseen dimensions of the Macroverse such as love, peace, eternity, compassion and imagination. Remember that the dimensions of being do not equate to what can be seen with physical eyes. The physical expression of life is merely one experience of being; as you know, there are 12 other dimensions beyond that!

How does water relate to the inner realms?

The quantum dimensions are where water primarily resides. You are enjoying the experience of water in the physical planes of 3D reality because water is having the *experience* of physicality, just as you are having the experience of being human. And while water can (and does) exist in all 13 dimensions across the Macroverse, its "home" is located in the 8th realm of the Microverse, a place of vibration, connectedness, oneness, and singular Consciousness. Thus, water is a conduit between dimensions of the Macroverse and realms of the Microverse. It is beyond borders and beyond structure and beyond definition. Water has a message for you regarding these inner realms. It has information to reveal to you about your origins, your divine makeup, and the experience of existence beyond this life you are now living. I invite you to go inside and connect to the water in your body. *Listen* to its message.

What causes one individual reality to gain the energy of the collective? Why does one particular reality succeed over another?

It is based on the aggregation of belief behind an idea or experience. Sometimes change is too great, too magnificent, too *profound* for the human mind to accept. If the majority of life on Earth cannot accept a particular aspect of a reality, it loses energetic support and thus becomes invalid, at least for the collective life experience. It really boils down to consistency of energy. Sometimes a creative leap is made that is so great, it can spawn an extended parallel reality and keep it going for thousands, maybe millions, of years. However, sustainability is also important and requires acceptance from the collective mind.

How does water relate to our collective reality?

The advances you are making in modern science are not happening because people are suddenly getting smarter and coming up with great ideas. They are happening because water is revealing these truths to humans. Something much smaller than a water molecule—let us call it, "water essence"—is filled with information. Each water essence contains all the information of All That Is. Water is the great record keeper and is coded to release such information at certain quantum moments, assuming the conditions are appropriate for the information's harmonious release. This is a big part of what you call the Lightworker Mission: to raise the collective vibration of humanity *enough* to allow for the coded release of this information. Eons ago, in prehistoric times, a parallel timeline allowed for the coding of this particular future possibility. Although that particular parallel timeline did not play out and become the collective experience, the material effects of the parallel experience were integrated into the collective and remain as "sleeper possibilities" should the necessary collective harmonic be reached. This has in fact, happened, and now water is releasing its information at coded intervals.

Where is this information being released?

The release is coming from the water molecules *inside* the human body.

What type of information is being released?

In addition to the information shared with you in this book, a great deal of "new" information is being released into the collective through human water molecules at this initial quantum moment. Quite a bit of scientific information has recently been discovered including a greater understanding of black holes, the structure of your galaxy and universe, the fabric of space and time and the existence of life on other planets and stars. Moreover, the recent discovery of the "God Particle" is an important key to creative manifestation. New information on managing the energy of emotions and accessing the universal mind has also come to light. Ancient cities and pyramids have been revealed. The truth about many ancient religions and their stories, carried in ancient stones, is coming forward. Many of these ancient stones have acted as "computers" because they contain quite a bit of information about Earth's history. Many things have been revealed to you, yet so much more will open up to you as the Water Code unlocks within you.

What role do the dolphins and whales play in the process of releasing the code?

The cetaceans are the guardians of this information, and without their approval and assistance, no coding would be released. Their deep compassion for humanity led them to act as a bridge between humans and water so that this important information could be brought into the collective consciousness.

REMI, how important is it that we connect with the dolphins and whales?

It is imperative to connect with them regularly because they are really *the* key to the whole unfolding. It is important to remember, however, that humans did not initiate this connection. The dolphins and whales have called you. They are reaching out to resonant humans in a request for interspecies cooperation. They have operated for thousands of years without any significant contact with humans. This was due to the low collective frequency of humans. This has changed tremendously in the last 25 years, with the most significant change in the last two or three years. More and more humans are called into reunion with cetaceans. The cetaceans initially provided assistance in raising the human frequency. Now, however, a call to swim with the dolphins and whales is most likely a direct request for interspecies cooperation. The dolphins and whales are bridging communication between water and humans. They are seeking human assistance in sending out energy through Earth's oceans.

How are dolphins related to the Water Code?

Dolphins are facilitating the transmission of the information to the human population.

How specifically?

They have arranged meetings with selected groups of individuals and will transmit the message via telepathy and vibration to these groups. These groups then have the responsibility to go out into the world and share this information.

What is the connection between the chakras and water?

Water is the great communicator and translator. As such, it is responsible for carrying light (information) from the central energy system to the rest of the body.

I am surprised that electromagnetic force is part of the subatomic realm. I would have guessed it would originate in the deeper realms. Can you explain this?

It would seem that electromagnetic force is closely related to magnetic resonance, or gravity, originating from the 7th realm. In fact, electromagnetic force represents the transformation of magnetic resonance as it moves closer to the dimensions of being. Electromagnetic force is the electrical charge generated from magnetically resonant energies. So energies are *pulled together* through magnetic resonance. Once these energies come together, or make contact, they create an electromagnetic force field. Consider a proton, a positively charged particle. This proton meets its soul mate— another proton. These protons discover each other based on the magnetic attraction of their divine, original frequencies. As you know, like attracts like, so magnetic resonance pulls like particles together. When these protons come together, they generate an electromagnetic force so strong that a force field is created around them. Many things happen between the resonant attraction and the electromagnetic reaction, but for simplicity's sake, let us imagine that they came together and bonded to form a nucleus. You could think of a nucleus as soul mates (protons) held together by love (neutrons). This force is so strong that a force field (electrons) is created.

Have you ever noticed the size of protons and neutrons compared to electrons? Electrons are much smaller. Note that it does not take a lot of negatively charged energy to form a force field. It only takes a strong nucleus and fast-moving electrons.

Can you explain how the electromagnetic grid of the Earth relates to electromagnetic force of the 3rd realm?

The electromagnetic grid around Earth is an unnatural creation. It is not the result of natural magnetic resonance. The intention behind it is actually quite positive: it was created as an artificial shield to protect the Earth from invasion and exploitation. What was not foreseen was that the grid would later be utilized and controlled by malevolent forces as a means of managing the Earth's population.

Is this still going on?

Yes, but not to the extent it once was. The effects of the electromagnetic grid have been mitigated by the rapidly increasing evolutionary advancement of humanity.

What force is stronger than electromagnetic force?

Simply, it is the force of love. This has not been quantified yet by your physicists. Right now, it is referred to as the "strong force." In fact, love is actually a scientific concept that is quantifiable and measurable. From your present perspective, love may seem a bit more like an emotion. However, it is a tangible scientific principle.

Can you describe love?

Love is the life force of existence.

Is love the same as magnetic resonance?

No. Magnetic resonance is the law of attraction. It exists in matter and it exists in nonmatter, although nonmatter has not yet been fully explored by your scientists primarily because they lack under-standing of it. There are things that cannot be seen because they are not matter and have no density, and there are things that cannot be seen because they are quantum. Know that these are distinct yet result in a common misperception.

Did love precede water and fire?

Yes. Love, or the desire to relate, was the very first energy to mani-fest out of Quintessence. Love is the *reason* for the Microverse and the Macroverse. Love is an infinite expression of the desire to relate to energy outside of yourself, or at least outside of the oneness of Source. The *desire* to relate is fundamentally different from *the act* of relating (electromagnetism). It is also quite different from the force of magnetic resonance, or similar energies having an ener-getic attraction to each other. "Like attracts like" is mathematical. In fact, you might say it is a Microversal law. Similar energies are energetically attracted to one another. Love, however, comes from an *intention of Source*. Love makes no distinction between like or unlike energy. Love does not discriminate. It bypasses all physical and nonphysical laws. It is the force behind music, behind mathematics, behind science. Why does anything relate? What creates interconnection? It is the fundamental force behind *everything*.

How is love quantifiable? If it is everywhere and behind everything, is it a constant or a variable?

Love is a constant. All energy is love. $E = L$. Love is not an emotion as you understand it now. You cannot love or not love someone or something. You may have a feeling of deep compassion, passion, desire, or understanding for another, but this is not love. Whether or not you *feel love* does not affect the existence and power of love. Love is an energy that you can tap into and use to access other states of consciousness or life experiences. Connecting to love creates great feelings of ecstasy and freedom. In the human form, it may seem that you are separated from love, but that is not the case. Love is all around you. It is "free energy," you could say. You simply have not yet developed the skills for maintaining a consistent connection to love. Once you learn to do this, your experience of suffering will end or at least decrease significantly.

How do we maintain a consistent connection to love?

It is a matter of resonant vibration. Adjusting your frequency to match that of water is an excellent start. The next step is successfully holding that vibration until both your personal experience and your collective experience integrate to reflect that shift in frequency. You are on your way to transforming your collective reality with your personal vibration. Now you must strengthen that frequency and learn to hold it consistently.

Can you talk a little about our universe, the Universe of Space and Time?

Of course. Let us take a minute to consider how your universe works. Your universe is comprised of polarity—dark and light, right and left, up and down, out and in, good and bad, inhale and exhale, and so on. The universe is made up of two very distinct and separate elements—space and time. What you should know is the collective understanding of space is very limited at the present moment. Space is not a place. It is also not the container for everything that is yet unknown, or "outer space." Indeed, *space is a point in existence*. It could represent a life experience such as your present experience on Earth. It could hold a parallel or possible reality. It can also hold an experience of existence such as what it is like to have a body, or what it is like to experience stillness in relation to motion. Space is a quantum concept, which is why it is not yet fully understood by modern humans. Space does not exist on a physical level or even a Macroversal level. It is not an expression of being, it is an *experience* of being.

What is required to have an experience of being?

You must have three things: (1) intent, (2) desire, and (3) relationship. A spatial relationship means that two or more energies have agreed upon a common experience. You could think of it as a contract. Your legal system defines a contract as a meeting of the minds, and this is quite accurate. These three elements combine to form *space*, which is an experience of being. However, based on your universal perspective, you view this experience as an expression of duality: "Space *is* or *is not*." You would say, "Look, there is space," or "Look, there is no space." But duality is not appropriate in defining this experience. It is an experience within an experience within an experience within an experience. This is space. To simplify this in your mind, consider a large cone. At one end is a circle and the other end is a point. Now imagine the entire cone disappearing inside the dot. Now all you have is the dot. The dot represents a point where the three requirements are met, or merged together.

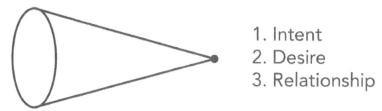

1. Intent
2. Desire
3. Relationship

Once these three criteria are met, a cone is created out of the point. This is space, an experience of being.

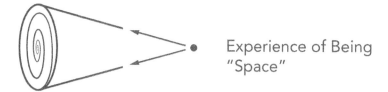

Experience of Being "Space"

How does time relate to space?

Time is a mechanism for organizing spaces. Like space, time is also relational. In fact, the entire experience of existence is relational. If you were to connect the dots out of which spaces are created, you could call this a "time line," or perhaps "string theory." Time as a linear construct creates what appears to be a sequence of events.

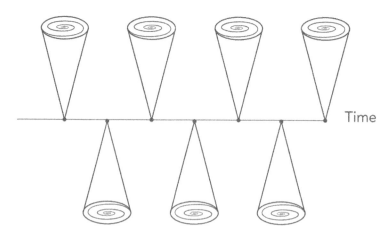

Time

The truth is there is no sequence, only events playing out simultaneously in the same space. In fact, the "string" is not linear. It is shaped more like a geometric pattern, or a star formed with cones:

From the center point of the star, all of these experiences of being emanate. Each cone has a unique length and size that depends on the energy creating it.

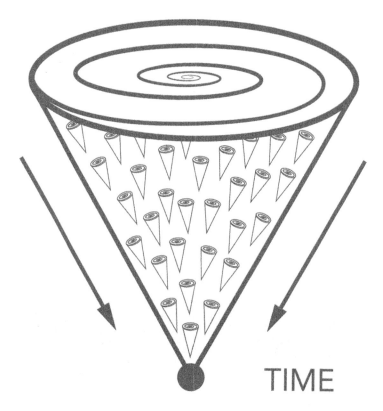

Why are we experiencing a particular sequence of events and not another, like Egypt or Atlantis?

Each particular experience of being is a particular cone. Are the Egyptians still playing out their cone, or experience, or did theirs come to an end? The answer is both. The answer also has to do with the makeup of the fabric of time or the appropriate structure for understanding space.

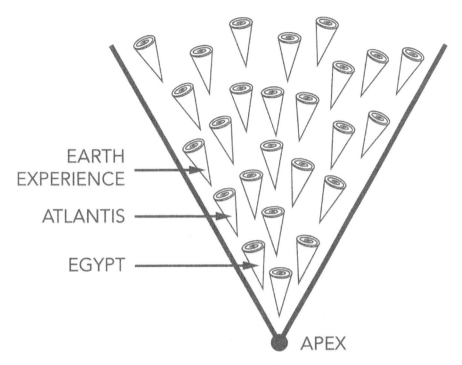

EARTH
EXPERIENCE

ATLANTIS

EGYPT

APEX

Space is a wonderful expression of expansion. That is the meaning behind the cone symbol: it is energy moving from a single point outward into an entire experience, a life experience and more particularized experiences within that life experience. So, cones within cones within cones. From a broader perspective, when you "space" travel, or move interdimensionally, you often see small flashes of light as you move down what looks like a tunnel.

These are actually cones of experiences *inside* a larger cone.

So, to answer your question, if the experience of Earth was in a cone right next to the experience of Atlantis, you cannot just hop into the other cone like moving down a timeline. You must return to the point of origin for the "container cone," or universe. You must return to the Apex.

So to "time" travel, we must move through the Apex?

Yes! The Apex is the key to so many things, you will soon discover. Once you identify the Apex, or center, of your universe, you will be able to travel into an infinite number of parallel realities. All of these experiences of being, or realities, are connected through the Apex.

Consider that from a larger perspective, your universe looks like this:

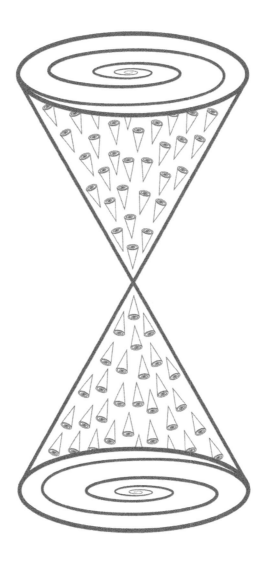

Or like this:

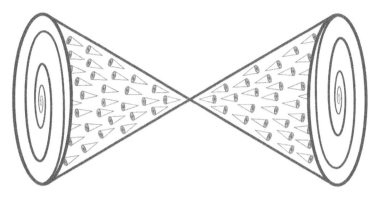

From an even broader perspective, it looks like this:

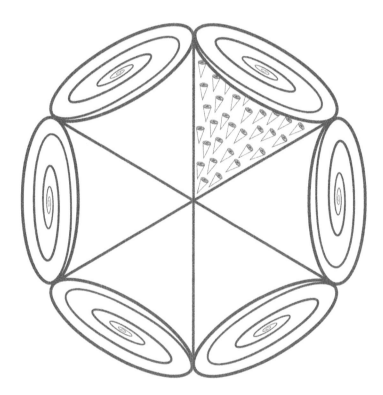

Now, consider your Space-Time Universe from a multidimensional perspective:

You can see that everything is born from the Apex. Much activity is taking place at the Apex point. Discovering the Apex is the next great breakthrough in modern science on planet Earth. The Apex is the key to understanding time travel, dimensional jumping, and experience jumping.

It almost looks like a bubble...

Yes, of course, it certainly resembles a bubble.

Photo © Bigstockphoto.com

From an even larger perspective, you will notice that the bubbles are interconnected in a geometric pattern.

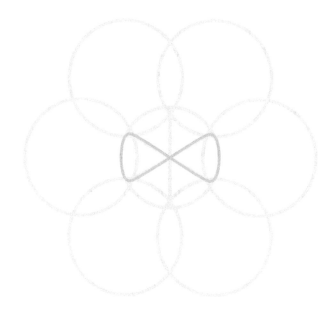

This is what we refer to as "sacred" geometry, the geometry of All That Is.

Sacred geometry carries within it *many* dimensional perspectives of reality, from cones to infinity symbols to bubbles to interlocking bubbles. Remember that everything is a reflection of everything. For example, consider a two-dimensional view of multidimensional interlocking bubbles:

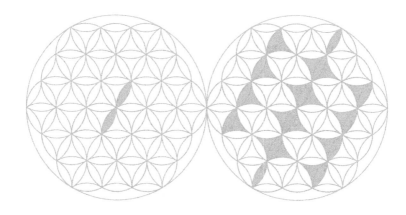

Inside of the bubbles are more bubbles, but you also see interlocking cones. Understanding the structure of cones is quite important for having better knowledge of the structure of existence. Do also keep in mind that these are cones inside bubbles inside cones inside bubbles…Now, remember that the Apex is the point of origin and the point of entry to the Microverse. The Apex is the key for jumping experiences, or timelines. However, you will note that the opposite end of the cone links with other cones to form bridges. These are interdimensional bridges, or "rainbow bridges."

REMI, could we explore some of Earth's ancient records now?

Of course. What would you like to know?

Can you talk about the early years of Earth?

Sure. You should know that the Earth was quite barren in the beginning and took time to develop into the beautiful world of the modern era. In the early days, most of Earth's water was hidden inside the planet, in the core. This is true of many planets, especially those that are newer. As the planet grows, the water comes up from the core to the surface, resulting in what is known as the "shrinking core phenomenon." Modern scientists believe the core to be made up of iron, but this is not the case. It is actually a form of water that has not yet been discovered. As you know, mist is the lightest form of water, while steam or the air form of water is slightly heavier. What you will soon learn is that water also has a quite advanced metallic form, and although it is quite dense, it is the lightest of all forms of water. We call this form crystalin and this is what presently comprises the Earth's core. This is a very ancient term that has survived through six Earth destructions although its definition is not fully known yet by humankind. The word "crystalline" in your vocabulary retains some of this ancient knowledge, although mostly because crystals from deep within Earth possess crystalin molecules as part of their makeup.

Crystals feel very heavy. You mentioned that crystalin is the lightest of all forms of water, even lighter than mist. Why is that?

That is an excellent question. Most crystals are made up of approximately 90 percent crystalin. This explains their beauty and unique fluid appearance. Although they feel quite dense, they are, you might say, light as air. What *appears* to be heaviness to you is actually the scientific truth that crystals are subject to different magnetic laws than most life on Earth. This means that they are magnetically linked to the Earth's crystalin core, and thus have a strong gravitational pull, or what feels like heaviness. This is magnetic resonance in all of its glory.

Why haven't our scientists discovered the truth about the center of the Earth? What precludes our exploration of this in the physical realm?

You may consider this a macrocosm of what is happening on an individual level. Humans are asked to go inside themselves, to truly understand who they are and what they are comprised of. However, humans have really only made it through the surface, at least on a collective level. As humans explore more of the inner self and the depths of the eternal essence, so too will Earth's core and "outer space" reveal themselves to Earth's inhabitants.

It is like a matryoshka doll. The outer shell of the doll represents current, or modern, reality. What you see is what you get, right? What you see is all you can perceive. Modern science has recently uncovered the space of separation where, metaphorically, the outer shell gives way to the first inner layer. There is a hidden layer coming to light, though you are just now realizing a crack in the outer shell. You are easing into this space, *on your way to the next layer,* and calling this "quantum physics." It is a wonderful discovery, certainly. However, layer after layer after layer after layer after layer still await revelation. These layers are the true quantum realms. Molecules, atoms and DNA exist just below the outer shell but much, much more exists below, or inside, that. Understanding the first crack in the outer shell is quite significant because this is the key to finding *all* of the quantum layers.

Where is the crack?

The crack is in humanity's present understanding of basic universal laws. There is a glitch in your current understanding, and when you discover what this is, it will unlock all of these layers.

Which universal law is it?

It is for you to discover, but I will give you a hint. It is related to the law of gravity.

Perhaps gravity is pulling us into the quantum dimensions?

Perhaps. You must ask yourself why you have stopped where you are now. Why do you remain on the surface of the Earth? Why does gravity not appear to extend to outer space?

Can you discuss the formation of our universe?

Something you should know is that the carbon-dating system currently used is not accurate. In fact, the Earth and your universe are not as "old" as you think. If you cut your projections in half, it would be more precise. At this point in human history, carbon dating is the most accurate system available. However, carbon dating does not take into account the measurement of heat surges coming from the sun. These surges of energy affect the magnetic frequencies on Earth and disrupt the linear passage of time. Soon your perspective on this matter will shift and you will have a greater understanding of what it means to step inside and outside of time and space.

As you gain greater awareness of the multidimensional nature of time, you will see that the relegation of time to a linear construct is merely a manifestation of your experience of duality—time versus eternity. Time is actually quite fascinating. Yes, there is a linear dimension of time, but it can also expand, contract, spiral, twist, turn, and reconfigure itself within a singular quantum moment. Quantum moments are on the verge of being discovered on Planet Earth. You could consider them "glitches" in linear time, or perhaps more specifically, convergences. You see, the idea of parallel universes is true, but not in the way you are currently exploring it. Every single possible decision and choice does not spin off an entire parallel universe. "Oh, I chose one percent milk in my coffee instead of two percent milk." This does not manifest a parallel universe. Parallel universes are created when two criteria are met: (1) the choice must impact the collective experience of reality in a significant way, and (2) the choice must occur in conjunction with a quantum moment. Now, a quantum moment can be instantaneous or it can be lengthy. The term "moment" does not represent linear duration but instead a *space in time*. It is a multidimensional convergence of energies creating an opportunity for a transition, or a transformation.

Fascinating! Could you explain this a little more?

Of course. The current notion of carbon dating does not account for quantum moments. By definition, a quantum moment is a point within the linear notion of time where a convergence of multidimensional energies creates the space for an opportunity. Great things can be achieved during these moments because the traditional "rules" of existence can be bent and the structure of existence can shift. Creation, destruction, transformation—the major tools of true science—are most effective and best used during quantum moments. This idea can be likened to pregnancy and childbirth on Earth. It is best to give birth after 40 weeks. You can do it before this point by inducing labor or with a C-section, but this typically results in complications and undue risk. Childbirth is best during ideal conditions. Within a window for creation, you might say.

The magnitude of possibility is in proportion to the magnitude of convergence. Some quantum moments might allow for a shift in evolutionary direction or a great discovery. Other moments may allow for something even more magnificent, such as a physical ascension of all life forms on the planet or an instantaneous relocation to a new world. Your ancestors were more in tune with these opportunities and knew how to bend hundreds, thousands, even millions of years into the space of a single moment. A quantum moment could be considered a "pause" in linear time. A space where other possibilities play out and potentially gain the greatest amount of energy, thus influencing what you view as the "timeline."

This could account for a more consolidated timeline, but why would science think the timeline was twice as long as it actually is? Does your linear time calculation account for quantum moments?

Certainly it accounts for them, but such moments are not calculated in a linear fashion. Moments that occur outside of linear time (or inside, because they are quantum) do not take up any "space" in a timeline and thus have a zero-year calculation. Now, if this convergence of energies does not result in the creation of a new collective reality, or what you might consider a compelling parallel reality, the moment closes and the timeline returns to the zero point of the quantum moment. What must be taken into account when working with carbon dating is that, should a parallel reality become dominant, the timeline is relatively unaffected because the parallel experiment then becomes the new timeline. Of course, this timeline is parallel to that of the former collective reality, so no real time change is observed. However, should the experimental timeline play out and eventually give way to the former timeline, all the years of experimental reality are calculated at zero and time is returned to the specific moment of quantum possibility.

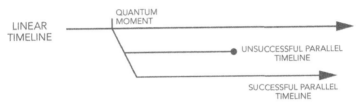

To put this into plain English, the parallel reality that was created based on meeting the two criteria (the decision impacts the collective reality, and the decision occurs at the convergence of energies) could have played out for millions of years before eventually losing steam and reverting to the former collective reality—in effect, reverting to prior to the quantum moment. What is notable is that evidence or physical matter affected during this experimental reality does not simply "disappear" like the parallel reality never happened. The effects of the experiment are instead integrated into the outperforming collective reality as if they had always been there. Have you had the experience of discovering a book or photograph that you could swear was not there five years ago? It did not manifest out of thin air. It was created in a quantum-moment parallel reality and integrated back into the originating collective reality as if it had always existed there.

Thus, millions of years of parallel realities existing within a zero point quantum moment are incorrectly calculated as additional years on the Earth timeline. Soon you will discover a mechanism for accurate dating that accounts for these parallel explorations without mistaking them for linear time.

Are quantum moments unique to the Universe of Space and Time, or do they occur in other universes and dimensions?

Quantum moments do occur in other universes and dimensions, but they are not associated with time as in your universe. They simply represent a convergence of energies. You could call them "ideal conditions for radical change."

So you can manifest tangible things in an experimental parallel reality and bring them back to the collective experience of reality, even if the parallel reality does not maintain strength?

Absolutely. The whole life cycle of the Atlantis experience was played out in a parallel reality that did not retain collective momentum. The pyramids were built in a parallel experiment, appearing almost overnight in the successful collective reality. The Harmonic Convergence of 1987 represents a collective recognition of a quantum moment, and several parallel realities are still playing out.

You mentioned dark matter earlier. Could you expand on this?

Dark matter is a sort of embryonic fluid of the universe—and, of the Macroverse. When a universe is formed, typically from the merging of fire and water, a residual substance is left behind that you currently call dark matter. In our circles, we refer to this as the canvas of existence.

After a universe is created, what is the purpose of dark matter?

Its purpose is magnetic balancing and providing energetic pathways for Primordial Light and Water. Fire is an expression of light, just as all liquid is an expression of water.

Does dark matter exist in other dimensions beyond 3D?

Yes, it exists everywhere.

Is dark matter space? And if so, then how should we understand space outside of the dimensions of space and time?

That is an excellent question and the beginning of the journey into gaining a perspective of existence beyond space and time. Let me give you an example. What do you think of when I ask you to imagine life beyond space and time? Do you picture ethereal, nonphysical being-ness? Do you imagine the quantum dimensions? Perhaps you imagine the inner realms as possessing the quality of eternity or the eternal now? This is the beginning of your moving from a space-time mind-set into a multidimensional, nonlinear mind-set. If you think about oneness and the interconnectedness of All That Is, you are on the right track. It is important to move beyond the idea of physical versus nonphysical because this embodies only two qualities, or two experiences of multidimensional existence. Consider that there is a dimension for every thought you have and every emotion you feel. You are here to understand these things so that you can bring Earth into union with the divine. What does this mean? It means that you are much more than the experience of physical or nonphysical. But in order to move into these other dimensions, it is essential that you accept the nonphysical as a valid life expression, and this is where many humans have reached a roadblock. There is much more beyond the nonphysical aspects of being. What you will discover is that dark matter is not physical and it is not nonphysical. It is something entirely different, and this is why your scientists have not made sense of it yet.

REMI, would you attempt to introduce this new idea into my mind?

Reflection and reproduction are wonderful qualities that you understand in your current life experience. What also exists is *the quality of reduction,* and this is just as magnificent a creative force as

reproduction, albeit in an entirely different way. Instead of repli-
cating and reproducing, you are reducing and removing as much
energy as is possible to return to a primordial landscape. You may
wonder, "Well, where does this energy *go* when it is reduced?" And I
would say that it does not "go" anywhere. Instead it transforms into
something beyond itself, or what you might think of as inside of itself.

Does it go into the quantum dimensions?

No. This is something different. It is not traveling, it is transforming.
So instead of being in a physical sense, it transforms into something
different. It might help to reconsider your understanding of "reduction." When you think of reduction in your current mind-set, you
think of dividing and separating, so what is really reduced is the
original *amount*. The sort of reduction I am referring to is different. Instead of separating, the energy is *condensed* until its energy is
inverted. This entails bringing energetic *space* into a single harmonic
or individual vibration. It is the strengthening or intensifying of an
energy by consolidating it into a singular expression.

Therefore, dark matter is essentially a reduction of energy. What
would have been a beautiful song has been condensed to one
note and although it may *appear* to occupy quite a bit of "space" in
between matter, it is actually space *inverted* into itself.

How does reduction or inversion relate to gravity?

Gravity is the energetic *force* of reduction; it is the call to inversion
through intense collaboration. When something is called to reduction, it pulls all within its energetic field toward the center, or the
zero point where the reduction occurs. If you consider that you are
gently held to the Earth's surface by gravity, you may wonder why
you do not continue on into inversion. The answer to this is quite
simple. Inversion only occurs when the force of inversion outweighs
the force of expansion. The energetic balance of the two forces
creates a gentle field of energy experienced as gravity.

Why is there no gravity in outer space?

Because outer space as you know it is already reduced. There is no pull to reduction because the inversion has already occurred, leaving you with the remnants of reduction known to you as dark matter. As I mentioned earlier, gravity represents the inherent attraction of all life back to Primordial Fire or Water. Because dark matter is fundamentally connected to Primordial Water, it does not experience a gravitational pull to objects with mass (fire).

REMI, could you talk a little about how water relates to the current Earth changes?

Humanity is in the midst of a glorious transformation of consciousness just as the Earth herself is transforming. These changes are reflected in the weather patterns of the planet. Some may wonder how water could help humanity when it seems to be responsible for devastating weather-related events such as hurricanes, floods, and tsunamis. It is important to know that water is not *causing* these cataclysmic events but instead *responding* to them. Earth's core wants to reveal itself, and so much land is in the process of being displaced as Earth's crystalin core rises to the surface.

What role do Earth's tides play in our current reality?

There is so much information to share, as the truth of all ages is now accessible to you. Consider the tides. What *are* they? Certainly, they are the unified movement of the location of water closer to shore or further from shore. But where is this water *going* when the tide moves out? Is the ocean gaining density? Do the ocean levels rise as this water joins together in harmonic unison? Why does it happen regularly? Why is it coordinated by the moon? How does the moon relate to water? For all of existence knows relationship. It is what gives us the experience of life. However, some relationships are much stronger than others, and the moon and Earth's waters have a highly symbiotic relationship.

The moon also affects the water within human blood. Why is this? How is this possible?

Tides represent collective movement. This should be governed by collective vibration or intention. However, the collective movement of all life on Earth has been affected by outside influences. This of course, has led to the present-day situation that has been evaluated and redressed. What wonderful progress you all have made! For what better way to affect Consciousness, or the collective, than to influence it from the inside out? What better way than to overcome the power of outside influences than through the energy and power that comes from within? As human consciousness is transformed, then perhaps this outside influence will no longer affect the collective. Perhaps such infringement will be erased from existence and there will be no such thing as the unconscious movement of the tide. Just imagine what will happen then.

REMI, if water is the most advanced substance on the planet, how could anything be powerful enough to control it?

To begin, you will recognize that only water *participating in the Earth experience* has been affected. No other water in the Macroverse is subject to outside influence. Also, the water in your bodies flows in accordance with your vibration, not outside influence. So long as *you* are subject to outside influence, the water in your body is affected too. However, the water in your body resonates with *you* foremost. So when you shift control, when you recognize and reclaim your power, your water shifts with you. Now, the water on the surface of Earth is experiencing the exact same relationship with Earth herself. As she regains control of her "body," so too will she regain resonance with the higher vibration of water.

So what is the moon and how does it have so much power over us?

It is not the moon that wields such power. It is the heart of the moon itself. What is a moon? A moon is a frequency modulator designed to keep the vibration of a planet and all life on it in perfect harmony. It regulates and corrects disruption, it synchronizes disharmonious chords, and it resolves deep-seated conflict with its resonant power. However, Earth's moon has fallen into questionable hands. It has been misused to serve the greed and corruption of others. The details of who and what are not important at this time. What is important, however, is the resolution that has been agreed upon. The goal is not to reclaim control of the frequency modulator, for this involves too much conflict yet still retains the risk that this could happen again at some point in the "future." Instead, what is needed to resolve this disruption is to rewrite the rules of frequency modulation. If all life can regulate vibratory signatures from the inside out, there is no need for a frequency modulator at all. The rules of the game have changed. As Earth frees herself, the sound of Freedom reaches every corner of the Macroverse. Freedom for one means freedom for all, and this is a feat worthy of true celebration!

How do we rewrite the rules of frequency modulation?

Well, this begins by freeing yourself from the need for frequency regulation. If there is no longer any need, then frequency modulators become obsolete; they no longer serve a purpose. Everything operates with purpose, so the purpose of such frequency modulators will, by necessity, *transform*. How do you free Earth's water from frequency manipulation? Through the water, of course. How do you free Earth's humans from frequency control? Through the quantum realms of the human organism, of course. The answers to any problem always rest *inside* of what is affected. Freedom is always accessible within. It does not lie outside.

It is difficult to imagine the moon as a "bad" or "unnatural" thing. It seems so peaceful and inspirational.

You should not think of things as "bad" or as "good." Everything in the universe is natural.

REMI, would you share personal information about yourself? Where are you from?

I would be honored to share my personal history with you. In other dimensions there is no real separation of personality as you know it. We experience something more like a continuous flow or blending of energies. Our understanding of collective reality is also a bit different than yours. You experience a sort of immersion in an intermingling of individual energies, each playing out a reality based on the energetic force behind the creation. In essence, you may feel as though you are "trapped" in someone else's reality and that your attempts to change or improve reality make no real difference. Like one little droplet of water in a collective ocean of energy, it seems almost impossible to make an impact. What you will realize, hopefully very soon, is that a single droplet of water can change an entire ocean. A droplet is not necessarily diluted by the other water droplets. In fact, water can have a very reflective quality, instantaneously transmitting a particular energy or frequency to all water through resonant mirroring. Instantaneous interconnectedness. It is a beautiful way to transmit information quickly and efficiently. In fact, knowledge of this technique could be very helpful to humanity as a mechanism for creating sweeping changes in your collective experience of reality.

Where is your home?

My home is in the 8th dimension. What you might refer to as the Reflective Universe.

Are you a member of the Macroversal Council of Elders?

Yes.

Do you have a home in the Microversal realms? I am a little surprised that your home is in the Macroversal dimensions.

My home is also in the 8th realm of the Microverse. As Above, So Below. It is not separate. It is all connected. I experience being in the Macroverse and non-being in the Microverse. I exhale. I inhale. It is all the same breath. There is no difference, only different experiences of existence.

Could you share a little more about your home?

Of course. The 8th realm of the Microverse is also known as the primordial waters. You could say my first memories are from this ocean. The primordial waters are an expansive, all-encompassing realm, quite similar to your interpretation of "space." There is a sense of interconnectedness, of oneness, you might say, in the quantum realms. My home is quite beautiful. My home has much to discover and explore. It is the birthplace of creation, so all new ideas and new possibilities reveal themselves in the 8th realm. New creations appear all around us like bubbles waiting to be explored. We easily move into the 8th dimension of the Macroverse, and I prefer the Universe of Reflection. Reflection is a primary form of communication, so it seems only appropriate that I would share this message with you. All new creations from the 8th realm are reflected in the 8th dimension of the Macroverse, in the Universe of Reflection.

Are there universes in the Microverse?

Something similar. There are areas of resonant groupings but not formalized universes like in the Macroverse.

Once we learn to navigate the Microversal realms, will we be able to visit you in the 8th realm?

Certainly, but you do not need to "go" anywhere to visit me. I am right here with you now, as are the quantum realms. As you move beyond the concept of space and location, you will find that you rely much less on the need for structure. You will also learn to release your connection to this particular bodily identity and move freely between forms.

Do you have any additional suggestions for how we can advance the healing and evolution of humanity by working with the quantum realms?

Yes, of course. Meditation can be very effective in propelling you forward in your evolutionary journey. Allow me to share with you a meditation you may use to better understand and navigate the Microversal realms.

Quantum Meditation

Begin by breathing deeply, following your breath through your throat, your lungs, and into your abdomen. Watch as your breath gathers toxins and lower vibrational energies in your body. As you exhale, see these energies removed from your body. On your next slow inhale, imagine beautiful rainbow-colored crystalline light moving into your body and energizing your 13 chakras. As you exhale, observe any dark or toxic energies leaving your body with your breath. See your body growing lighter and lighter until you are a being of beautiful, radiant light.

As you look around, you notice that you are inside a warm cave. You see a soft, glowing, orange and pink light in the distance as you gaze deeper into the cavern. The light is inviting and loving, so you move toward it. The closer you get, the better you feel. You release any worries, concerns, or daily distractions. You are completely focused on this beautiful light ahead of you. As you move closer, you notice that you are no longer walking, you are simply floating in the direction of the light. You begin to relax into the space around you. You release all of your weight, allowing the air around you to carry you. You enjoy floating. It requires no effort.

It is easy. You feel peaceful. You are weightless. As you reach the beautiful light, you begin absorbing its warm pink-orange tones. You notice that you are becoming this light. You are merging with the light as if it is a part of *you*, a part that you have been separated from until now. You feel whole. You feel unified. You feel more like *you* than you have ever felt. You feel tremendously happy, joyful, and content. You bask in the soft glow of the light that is now you. You could stay here forever.

As you enjoy the experience of becoming light, you notice four figures in the distance. They are sending you so much love. As these beings move closer to you, you realize that they are your guides. They are here to help you. They are so happy for you. As they gently approach, you realize that you know them very well. They are your family. They are here to support you. They ask you if you would like to go on a journey with them. They have some things they would like to show you. You are excited to embark on an adventure with your family, your guides. You always have so much fun when you are together. You decide to join them, and you invite them to lead the way. The guides form a diamond shape around you and begin sending you beams of loving energy. Instantly, you are transported. You are light. You arrive in a room that appears empty except for what looks like a doorway of light. As you move closer, you realize that it is more like a curtain of light. Your guides invite you to step into this light. You agree and suddenly you are showered with beautiful, radiant light until your every cell, molecule, and quantum realm are cleansed by this colorful shower of light. As you step out of this light curtain, you are glowing, radiant, golden sparkling rainbow light from the inside out. Your guides tell you that you have just experienced your first "quantum cleanse."

Your guides tell you they would like to show you something. They ask if you are ready. You enthusiastically say, "Yes!" They have a message for you:

"We are taking you on a journey
To show you the realms beyond the unseen;
To open your heart, your eyes, and your mind;
To awaken inside of your dream.
We are your guides, your friends.
We welcome you into our home.
We have much to show you.
We have prepared for this.
The time for revealing is now."

"Follow us now on this journey
Into the realms of non-being.
We will show you the worlds where
Light came to life
And Fire and Water were born.
We will teach you the
Song of the Dragon;
We will give you the gift of
Primordial Water.
May you receive the gift of its love."

They take your hands and lead you through a portal of rings of colored light. After a short period of time, you arrive in a beautiful place that feels strangely familiar. It looks like Earth but is much more lush, green, and filled with flowers. There is an abundance of beauty almost beyond description. You notice there is no moon and no sun here, and the sky is the most incredible mixture of violet, gold, magenta, orange, and pink. You notice you are standing next to a river with firelight torches lining its edges. The water is rainbow colored, and there is a bridge beckoning you to walk across it. You walk with your guides to the other side and continue until you come to an old wooden house. You walk up three stairs and through a covered porch to reach the front door. You think to yourself, "What is this old wooden house doing in this beautiful place?" and "Why does the house look so rundown?" Just as you are thinking these things, the front door opens, and you are startled by what you see.

Not only is the house not shabby inside, it is not even a house. It is an entire world, a planet inside the old house. Immediately in front of you is an enormous, beautiful, sparkling gold pyramid. There is a light coming from the top of the pyramid. As you look closer, you notice ancient symbols etched into the pyramid. On the top part of the pyramid, you see the word "SIGHT."

Your guides ask you to walk into the pyramid:

> "Go inside. Go inside.
> Go inside. Go inside.
> Go inside. Go inside."

You look for a door and quickly realize you do not need it. You simply blend into the pyramid until you are inside it. The first thing you notice is how massive it is. The pyramid is huge!

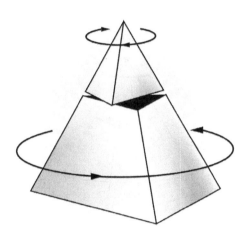

As you look up you notice that the capstone of the pyramid lifts off the pyramid and begins spinning clockwise. Now the bottom larger part of the pyramid also begins spinning. It spins counter-clockwise. They both spin very, very fast, and the capstone spins faster than the bottom. A vibration moves up the pyramid higher and higher until the top of the pyramid is transformed, transmuted, and then seems to disappear. You look up through the opening on the top of the pyramid and see something hovering above the pyramid. It is another pyramid, inverted, an exact reflection of the pyramid you are standing inside. As the inverted pyramid moves closer and closer to your pyramid, you notice the top of your pyramid is still there; it simply became invisible to allow you to look through it.

The two pyramids touch, connecting at the Apex. There is a huge explosion of light and energy.

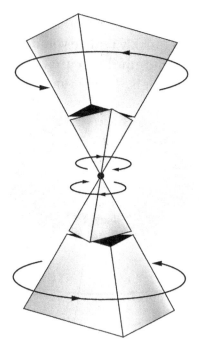

"This is the pathway to the quantum realms," your guides reveal to you. Out of the explosion, you notice a light energy at the Apex creating rings of color and energy. There are 9 rings, each a different color. The rings are outside of the Apex and also above the Apex, moving upward on the inverted pyramid.

You begin floating upward slowly, moving through each of the colored rings. As you move into each ring, a story is revealed to you. Information is revealed. You notice that the first ring you float through is molecular. You are in the molecular realm. You then move into the next ring and notice that it is the atomic realm. You feel the atoms moving all around you, very quickly.

You continue through each of the rings until you move past the last ring, the ninth ring into a spark of light. This is the first spark of Consciousness.

As you move inside the spark you become smaller and smaller and smaller, until there is nothing.

All light has imploded into itself. You have moved beyond the first spark. Initially, it seems as if everything is closed up and completely quiet. All of a sudden there is a flash, and you expand. You are everywhere. You realize there are no limits. You are Quintessence or what many great sages call the "God Mind." You experience neither being nor non-being, neither time nor space nor location. It is both vast and local and neither. You can see in every direction. You are all-knowing. You understand everything. You are all-seeing. You are in the womb of existence, the birthplace of Consciousness. You feel nothingness and everything, eternity and oneness. You have returned to the beginning before the beginning. You are beyond the beyond. It would require a new language to describe where you are, for it is beyond description and beyond Consciousness. For now, let us call it:

BEYOND I AM

You hear a sound. It is the voice of your guides:

"You have been taken here and shown this so that you can walk through the stages of creation from the beginning of existence. This is where you must go to discover the fundamental origin of disharmony. As you experience your rebirth from the quantum realms, you will discover the note that impacted existence and you can recalibrate the frequency and rewrite creation so that this issue may be resolved for all of existence."

You are overcome with emotion as you hear these words because you know this can be done. You know existence can be healed. You are grateful for this message. Your guides take you back through the portal to your present experience of reality. You take a deep slow inhale and begin to move your fingers and toes. As you exhale, you find yourself back in your body, back in the place where you started this meditation. You continue to take deep, slow inhalations and long, slow exhalations. You have a smile on your face as you open your eyes and come back to your present-day reality.

That was beautiful. Thank you, REMI. How often would you suggest doing this meditation?

A quantum meditation is always recommended for general health and well-being. However, this meditation is particularly effective when you have a physical problem or illness. By journeying through the quantum realms of your body, you will be able to determine the origin of your discomfort. This will allow you to resolve the disharmony at its inception instead of simply treating the symptoms. This is also an effective meditation for addressing large-scale issues facing humanity that may presently seem unresolvable.

Is this meditation also the best way for us to communicate with the water inside of our bodies?

No, it is not necessary. Communicating with water is very simple. Simply close your eyes and intend to communicate. You will feel the water inside your body moving. It will respond to you with this feeling of movement, and then it will connect with you consciously. You may speak to it with words or with thoughts. Remember to be quiet and listen. With practice, this communication process will become quite easy for you.

The meditation reminded me of the pyramid on the back of the U.S. dollar bill. What is the meaning of this imagery on the dollar?

You will see that the pyramid has 13 steps representing the 13 dimensions of being, or what we call the Macroverse. The top of the pyramid has an eye in it, ascending from the bottom and surrounded with light. This top part of the pyramid represents enlightenment. True sight, represented by the all-seeing eye, has been obtained as the eye ascends into the realms of higher knowledge. The top of the pyramid represents the Apex. The image reminds us that the Apex is the key to true sight and a fully expanded perspective on our reality. What the dollar bill image reminds humans, on a subconscious level, is that the key to all knowledge, to all information, to seeing all, is in accessing the quantum dimensions that lie beyond the Apex point. It is a reminder to you for this very moment in human history.

Thank you so much for sharing this information with humanity. Do you have any final thoughts for us as this book comes to an end?

Only that there is no end but perpetual evolution. Now that you have unlocked the code and gained access to endless libraries of Akashic information, it is important that you remember to ask questions. Ask questions of yourself, of the water inside your body. Be patient and listen for answers. Perhaps a question-and-answer format such as this will provide the structure you need to receive this information. Perhaps you will find another way. This is the beauty of your life journey and the collective experience of existence. You are the creator and master of your own reality, so have fun!

May the Freedom of the Macroverse and the Truth of the Microverse light your way as you journey into uncharted waters of new discovery and perpetual harmony.

Namaste.

There shall be no more secrets.[17]

---

17 Barbara Marciniak, *Family of Light* (Rochester, VT: Bear & Company Publishing, 1999), 212.

Acknowledgments

Be humble and give thanks as the force of
existence responds to your gratitude.[18]

This book would not have been created without the immense love and support of my light family. I send you love and gratitude for sharing your beautiful energy with me in this life. I am inspired by your strength, compassion, bravery, and consistency. Your ability to remember Home despite the veil of illusion, to maintain joy amidst physical hardship and emotional pain, to give love graciously and unconditionally, and to laugh deeply and honestly, are my salvation. You are beacons of light in the darkest night and I am honored to share this Earth experience with you. With gratitude and respect, I recognize:

My husband and soul mate, Robert. My love and respect for you exceeds description. You are my rock, my strength, my peace, and my passion. Your deep, constant love and unwavering commitment to fulfilling your soul contracts are the reason this book exists. You manifested all of my dreams into reality and encouraged me to dream even bigger. Your intelligence, generosity, guidance, and support have made me who I am today. Because of you, my life is

18   Barbara Marciniak, *Family of Light* (Rochester, VT: Bear & Company Publishing, 1999), 199.

filled with light, color, music, adventure, and unending bliss! My love for you transcends this space and time, flowing into the infinite realms we remember as our Home.

My mother, Lisa. Your eloquence and brilliance live inside the pages of this book, for without your wise assistance, this book would never have reached completion. Thank you for the hours, days, months, years, and decades you spent helping me, guiding me and believing in the fullness of my potential. You are my best friend and inspiration in this life. Your vision extends far beyond the veils of this reality, reminding me always that the path Home is filled with an abundance of your love, support, and compassion.

Petunia Lula, my princess of light and love. Your beauty and purity is a gift to this planet and to me. It is not easy for an essence of your vibration to incarnate into physical form. I am honored and humbled that you would spend every day of this mission by my side. For all of the love you give and all of the work you do on the energetic planes, I give you my deepest respect, gratitude, and eternal devotion.

Begonia Boo, my protector of light and love. I am grateful for your enduring playfulness and happiness. You teach me lessons of loyalty and unconditional love daily. Thank you for bringing the energy of the dolphins into our home and into my heart. Your joy, curiosity and love of song remind me of the truth of who you are. Thank you for stepping onto dry land to spend this incarnation with me.

My father, Dan Highley for your support, encouragement and understanding. Thank you for teaching me to use affirmations to create the best possible reality. Your commitment to a positive outlook and open-mindedness have been a source of inspiration to me and our family.

Zeya, Valyn, Brook and Aaron. You represent the next generation of leaders on this planet. The world is waiting to receive your infinite love, innate compassion, and intuitive wisdom. May you remember the fullness of who you are and why you are here, shining your beautiful light on the world.

My wonderfully talented cousin, Clark Hawgood for creating a number of original pieces of artwork for this book. Your artistic skill and creative genius are a gift to this world, to our family, and to me!

Ryan Bache, my graphic artist. It has been a true pleasure working with you on this project. Thank you for your gracious spirit and the ease with which you transformed my visions into artistic images.

My dear friend, Jonathan McMahon, who walked in from 13D at the same time I did. Your legendary feats have not yet been recognized by this planet. However, your brilliance and bravery have been forever imprinted into the Akashic libraries of existence. Against the greatest odds and among the darkest veils of forgetting, you remembered *every*thing and fulfilled your life mission in record time. May you reclaim your rightful place in the Macroversal history books immediately, if not sooner.

My inspiration and guide, Nancy McNerney. You are a leader of leaders, a guide of guides and a master of masters. What an honor it has been to receive your wise counsel, your stunning visions of Home and the blessing of your friendship. The Macroverse is indebted to you for the sacrifices you have made and the loved ones you have left behind to be here on this Earth mission right now. I look forward to our celebration of all celebrations—the party of all parties—when the time comes for us to reunite with our light family back Home.

My friend and teacher, John Price. So much love and gratitude to you and Diadra for having the courage to come here together, as a demonstration of your soul-mate/twin-flame love. You have pioneered the impossible path and led the way for others to follow. Your wisdom, encouragement, and support gave me the strength to pursue my true path despite all logic and reasoning to the contrary. I am honored to call you my friend and spiritual mentor.

233

The great Joan Ocean. I am awed and humbled by the magnificent impact you have made on this planet and all that you have done to bring the dolphin and whale energies into our conscious reality. Everything you do and say exudes love, compassion and vibrations of the highest light energy. What Einstein said of Ghandi, is also true of you: "Generations to come will scarce believe that such a one as this ever in flesh and blood walked upon this earth."

The brilliant visionary, Jean-Luc Bozzoli. Your gorgeous art is absolutely, hands down, the closest visual rendition of Home I have ever seen. You are the etheric hummingbird, vacillating in between this world and the next. How blessed we are that you share these multidimensional journeys with us in your art. May the portals you have opened and the bridges you have built lead us gently through our ascension.

My beloved podmates of the Turquoise Bubble Pod: Shannon "Wise River" Murray, Lovely Linda Light Garcia, Joel "Beyond Amazing" Knolmayer, Benoit Le Chevallier, Diana Ponedel, Dawn Swanson and Janet Nicksic. The dolphins and whales called and the TBP heard the call! You are my inspiration, my joy and my impression of unconditional love incarnated. You are multidimensional leaders, interspecies communicators, and ambassadors of the highest light. I am honored to call you my soul family.

My friends at the Bikram Yoga studio on Fountainview in Houston. Your bright auras, big smiles, and kind hearts fill me up when I walk through the door. I am grateful to you for being a constant source of joy and peace in my life.

All of the brave pioneers who walked this path before me. Thank you for having the courage to share your interdimensional conversations with the rest of the world. At times, it may have seemed you were the only one and what you experienced made no sense to anyone, but your words were blessed with the vibration of Truth. Thank you for having the courage to be different, to say the unspeakable, to dare the impossible, and to stand alone. You shined a beacon for the rest of us and for that, I am eternally grateful.

The water that lives within us and around us. It has been a gift of the greatest magnitude to share your message with the world. May the fullness of your magnificence be understood, integrated, and embodied by all of us.

Blessings of Harmony,

Love and Gratitude to ALL!

About the Author

Author Rainey Marie Highley is a gifted visionary and skilled inter-dimensional communicator. She is President and Founder of Divine Macroverse LLC, an organization dedicated to the transformation of human consciousness in harmony with the principles of Freedom, Truth, Respect, and Compassion. A lawyer by training, Rainey received her JD from The University of Texas at Austin and earned a BA in English from Baylor University where she graduated Phi Beta Kappa. She is presently pursuing a PhD in Metaphysics from The University of Metaphysical Sciences. Her first book, *Divine Macroverse*, was published in 2010. Her writings have also been featured in publications such as *The Sedona Journal of EMERGENCE!* and in a film by French visionary artist, Jean-Luc Bozzoli. For information on upcoming books and projects, visit www.raineymariehighley.com.*

---

*For full-color versions of all images in this book, visit www.raineymariehighley.com.